Product Liability

POINT COUNTERPOINT

Affirmative Action

Amateur Athletics

American Military Policy

Animal Rights

Bankruptcy Law

Blogging

Capital Punishment,
Second Edition

Disaster Relief

DNA Evidence

Educational Standards

Election Reform

Energy Policy

Environmental Regulations
and Global Warming

The FCC and Regulating
Indecency

Fetal Rights

Food Safety

Freedom of Speech

Gay Rights

Gun Control

Hate Crimes

Immigrants' Rights After 9/11

Immigration Policy, Second
Edition

Juvenile Justice

Legalizing Marijuana

Mandatory Military Service

Media Bias

Mental Health Reform

Miranda Rights

Open Government

Physician-Assisted Suicide

Policing the Internet

Prescription and
Non-prescription Drugs

Prisoners' Rights

Private Property Rights

Product Liability

Protecting Ideas

Regulating Violence in
Entertainment

Religion in Public Schools

The Right to Die

The Right to Privacy

Rights of Students

Search and Seizure

Smoking Bans, Second Edition

Stem Cell Research and Cloning

Tort Reform

Trial of Juveniles as Adults

The War on Terror,
Second Edition

Welfare Reform

White-Collar Crime

Women in the Military

Product Liability

Victoria Sherrow

SERIES EDITOR
Alan Marzilli, M.A., J.D.

An imprint of Infobase Publishing

Product Liability

Chelsea House
An imprint of Infobase Publishing
132 West 31st Street
New York, NY 10001

Library of Congress Cataloging-in-Publication Data

Sherrow, Victoria.
 Product liability / by victoria sherrow, Alan Marzilli.
 p. cm. — (Point/counterpoint)
 Includes bibliographical references and index.
 ISBN 978-1-60413-509-1 (hardcover)
 1. Products liability—United States—Juvenile literature. I. Marzilli, Alan. II. Title. III. Series.

 KF8925.P7S54 2010
 346.7303'8—dc22

                                    2009029617

Chelsea House books are available at special discounts when purchased in bulk quantities for businesses, associations, institutions, or sales promotions. Please call our Special Sales Department in New York at (212) 967-8800 or (800) 322-8755.

You can find Chelsea House on the World Wide Web at http://www.chelseahouse.com.

Text design by Keith Trego
Cover design by Alicia Post
Composition by EJB Publishing Services
Cover printed by Bang Printing, Brainerd, MN
Book printed and bound by Bang Printing, Brainerd, MN
Date printed: March 2010
Printed in the United States of America

10 9 8 7 6 5 4 3 2 1

This book is printed on acid-free paper.

All links and Web addresses were checked and verified to be correct at the time of publication. Because of the dynamic nature of the Web, some addresses and links may have changed since publication and may no longer be valid.

Foreword	6
INTRODUCTION	
Product Liability in America	11
POINT	
Federal Liability Laws Are Needed	33
COUNTERPOINT	
Federal Liability Laws Are Unnecessary	45
POINT	
Strict Liability Standards Cause Economic Problems	55
COUNTERPOINT	
Strict Liability Standards Protect People	71
POINT	
Courts Should Have Less Discretion in Awarding Damages	80
COUNTERPOINT	
Courts Should Have Discretion in Awarding Damages	93
CONCLUSION	
Debates Go On	105
Appendix: Beginning Legal Research	121
Elements of the Argument	124
Notes	129
Resources	136
Picture Credits	144
Index	145

Alan Marzilli, M.A., J.D.
Birmingham, Alabama

The POINT/COUNTERPOINT series offers the reader a greater understanding of some of the most controversial issues in contemporary American society—issues such as capital punishment, immigration, gay rights, and gun control. We have looked for the most contemporary issues and have included topics—such as the controversies surrounding "blogging"—that we could not have imagined when the series began.

In each volume, the author has selected an issue of particular importance and set out some of the key arguments on both sides of the issue. Why study both sides of the debate? Maybe you have yet to make up your mind on an issue, and the arguments presented in the book will help you to form an opinion. More likely, however, you will already have an opinion on many of the issues covered by the series. There is always the chance that you will change your opinion after reading the arguments for the other side. But even if you are firmly committed to an issue—for example, school prayer or animal rights—reading both sides of the argument will help you to become a more effective advocate for your cause. By gaining an understanding of opposing arguments, you can develop answers to those arguments.

Perhaps more importantly, listening to the other side sometimes helps you see your opponent's arguments in a more human way. For example, Sister Helen Prejean, one of the nation's most visible opponents of capital punishment, has been deeply affected by her interactions with the families of murder victims. By seeing the families' grief and pain, she understands much better why people support the death penalty, and she is able to carry out her advocacy with a greater sensitivity to the needs and beliefs of death penalty supporters.

The books in the series include numerous features that help the reader to gain a greater understanding of the issues. Real-life examples illustrate the human side of the issues. Each chapter also includes excerpts from relevant laws, court cases, and other material, which provide a better foundation for understanding the arguments. The volumes contain citations to relevant sources of law and information, and an appendix guides the reader through the basics of legal research, both on the Internet and in the library. Today, through free Web sites, it is easy to access legal documents, and these books might give you ideas for your own research.

Studying the issues covered by the POINT/COUNTERPOINT series is more than an academic activity. The issues described in the books affect all of us as citizens. They are the issues that today's leaders debate and tomorrow's leaders will decide. While all of the issues covered in the POINT/COUNTERPOINT series are controversial today, and will remain so for the foreseeable future, it is entirely possible that the reader might one day play a central role in resolving the debate. Today it might seem that some debates—such as capital punishment and abortion—will never be resolved.

However, our nation's history is full of debates that seemed as though they never would be resolved, and many of the issues are now well settled—at least on the surface. In the nineteenth century, abolitionists met with widespread resistance to their efforts to end slavery. Ultimately, the controversy threatened the union, leading to the Civil War between the northern and southern states. Today, while a public debate over the merits of slavery would be unthinkable, racism persists in many aspects of society.

Similarly, today nobody questions women's right to vote. Yet at the beginning of the twentieth century, suffragists fought public battles for women's voting rights, and it was not until the passage of the Nineteenth Amendment in 1920 that the legal right of women to vote was established nationwide.

What makes an issue controversial? Often, controversies arise when most people agree that there is a problem but disagree about the best way to solve it. There is little argument that poverty is a major problem in the United States, especially in inner cities and rural areas. Yet, people disagree vehemently about the best way to address the problem. To some, the answer is social programs, such as welfare, food stamps, and public housing. However, many argue that such subsidies encourage dependence on government benefits while unfairly penalizing those who work and pay taxes, and that the real solution is to require people to support themselves.

American society is in a constant state of change, and sometimes modern practices clash with what many consider to be "traditional values," which are often rooted in conservative political views or religious beliefs. Many blame high crime rates, and problems such as poverty, illiteracy, and drug use on the breakdown of the traditional family structure of a married mother and father raising their children. Since the "sexual revolution" of the 1960s and 1970s, sparked in part by the widespread availability of the birth control pill, marriage rates have declined, and the number of children born outside of marriage has increased. The sexual revolution led to controversies over birth control, sex education, and other issues, most prominently abortion. Similarly, the gay rights movement has been challenged as a threat to traditional values. While many gay men and lesbians want to have the same right to marry and raise families as heterosexuals, many politicians and others have challenged gay marriage and adoption as a threat to American society.

Sometimes, new technology raises issues that we have never faced before, and society disagrees about the best solution. Are people free to swap music online, or does this violate the copyright laws that protect songwriters and musicians' ownership of the music that they create? Should scientists use "genetic engineering" to create new crops that are resistant to disease and pests and produce more food, or is it too risky to use a laboratory to create plants that nature never intended? Modern medicine has continued to increase the average lifespan—which is now 77 years, up from under 50 years at the beginning of the twentieth century—but many people are now choosing to die in comfort rather than living with painful ailments in their later years. For doctors, this presents an ethical dilemma: should they allow their patients to die? Should they assist patients in ending their own lives painlessly?

Perhaps the most controversial issues are those that implicate a Constitutional right. The Bill of Rights—the first 10 Amendments to the U.S. Constitution—spells out some of the most fundamental rights that distinguish our democracy from other nations with fewer freedoms. However, the sparsely worded document is open to interpretation, with each side saying that the Constitution is on their side. The Bill of Rights was meant to protect individual liberties; however, the needs of some individuals clash with society's needs. Thus, the Constitution often serves as a battleground between individuals and government officials seeking to protect society in some way. The First Amendment's guarantee of "freedom of speech" leads to some very difficult questions. Some forms of expression—such as burning an American flag—lead to public outrage, but are protected by the First Amendment. Other types of expression that most people find objectionable—such as child pornography—are not protected by the Constitution. The question is not only where to draw the line, but whether drawing lines around constitutional rights threatens our liberty.

The Bill of Rights raises many other questions about individual rights and societal "good." Is a prayer before a high school football game an "establishment of religion" prohibited by the First Amendment? Does the Second Amendment's promise of "the right to bear arms" include concealed handguns? Does stopping and frisking someone standing on a known drug corner constitute "unreasonable search and seizure" in violation of the Fourth Amendment? Although the U.S. Supreme Court has the ultimate authority in interpreting the U.S. Constitution, its answers do not always satisfy the public. When a group of nine people—sometimes by a five-to-four vote—makes a decision that affects hundreds of millions of others, public outcry can be expected. For example, the Supreme Court's 1973 ruling in *Roe v. Wade* that abortion is protected by the Constitution did little to quell the debate over abortion.

Whatever the root of the controversy, the books in the POINT/ COUNTERPOINT series seek to explain to the reader the origins of the debate, the current state of the law, and the arguments on either side of the debate. Our hope in creating this series is that readers will be better informed about the issues facing not only our politicians, but all of our nation's citizens, and become more actively involved in resolving these debates, as voters, concerned citizens, journalists, or maybe even elected officials.

This volume covers an area of the law that allows purchasers of defective or dangerous consumer goods to sue the companies that manufactured or sold them. Some believe that product liability laws help protect the public by encouraging manufacturers to design and test products wisely. They say that generous monetary awards are necessary, both to compensate consumers for their losses and to make producing unsafe products more expensive than producing safe products. Critics of current standards, however, disagree, arguing that greedy people and their attorneys too often exploit the laws, and that the mere threat of lawsuits increases the cost of doing business. The costs of defending and paying for frivolous lawsuits, these critics believe, are passed on to innocent consumers.

One area of controversy is the creation of a uniform federal law because product liability laws vary from state to state, even though many manufacturers sell their goods nationwide. Critics fear that such a law would rob states of the ability to protect their citizens adequately. Two areas in which laws might differ from jurisdiction to jurisdiction are the extent to which strict liability applies and standards for punitive damages. Under strict liability, the person bringing the lawsuit can recover money without proving that the manufacturer or seller failed to use care in manufacturing, inspecting, or selling the item—simply proving harm is enough. Jurisdictions also differ in their standards for awarding punitive damages—money that is assessed in order to punish the manufacturer or seller in cases of deliberate or reckless wrongdoing. The discussions in this volume will help to illuminate why products often carry seemingly ridiculous warning labels—like the coffee cup's warning that its contents are hot.

Product Liability in America

A lawsuit involving a 49-cent cup of coffee made news headlines in 1994. In February 1992, 79-year-old Stella Liebeck went through a McDonald's drive-through restaurant in Albuquerque with her grandson, who was driving the car. After he pulled over, she opened the cup to add cream and sugar but spilled the coffee on herself. Mrs. Liebeck suffered significant third-degree burns and was hospitalized for eight days. Her medical treatment, involving painful treatments and skin grafts, would continue for two years.

A jury in New Mexico awarded Mrs. Liebeck $200,000 in compensatory damages to compensate her for her injury and expenses. It also awarded her $2.7 million in punitive damages to punish McDonald's for harming her. Later, the $200,000 was reduced to $160,000 because the jury determined she was 20 percent at fault. The punitive damages award also was cut to

$480,000; eventually the two parties settled for an undisclosed amount.

To reach a decision in a case like this, the jury hears arguments from the plaintiff (person bringing the suit) and the defendant (company being sued). The Liebeck jury looked at the extent of the injury and how it occurred, and they considered whether McDonald's intended to cause the injury or could have predicted and/or prevented it. The plaintiff's attorneys said the temperature of the coffee was 40 to 50 degrees hotter than a person would expect—and also hotter than the prevailing industry standard. McDonald's served its coffee between 180–190 degrees Fahrenheit. At that temperature, argued Liebeck's attorney, coffee is not suitable for drinking. The plaintiff conceded that people expect coffee to be served hot, but she noted that this coffee was hot enough to cause third-degree burns within a few seconds. The plaintiff said the restaurant could have served its coffee at a lower temperature that was still hot enough to satisfy customers, and that it also should warn people that the coffee was hot enough to cause severe burns. The plaintiff presented evidence showing that during the previous 10 years more than 700 other people had reported being burned after spilling the coffee.[1]

This case sparked fierce debates. Mrs. Liebeck's supporters said the ruling showed that the law protects consumers from potentially dangerous products. They said that McDonald's should have reduced the temperature of its coffee, especially after so many people were burned, and that it should have posted larger warnings about the dangers of being burned from such hot coffee. Supporters further noted that Mrs. Liebeck initially requested a settlement of just $20,000, but the company refused. The supporters said that a high punitive damages award was needed to persuade McDonald's to serve coffee at a temperature that was safer for consumers.

Critics of the court's decision believed the case revealed serious flaws in the legal system, including the potential for excessive

At left, Stella Liebeck of Albuquerque, New Mexico, attends a news conference with her daughter Judy Allen in Washington, D.C., in March 1995. Liebeck became famous when a jury awarded her $2.7 million in damages after a hot cup of coffee from McDonald's spilled in her lap and burned her.

awards. Such laws put too-high burdens on businesses without requiring enough caution and care from consumers. Some called it yet another case of a "runaway jury" with an antibusiness bias. Critics also pointed out that many restaurants served their coffee as hot as McDonald's. Billions of customers handled the same coffee without being burned, and McDonald's did post a warning saying the coffee was hot. They noted that Mrs. Liebeck's injuries were especially serious because she was wearing a cotton sweat suit. This material absorbed the coffee, which burned her skin before she could wipe it off.

A few years later, a court in Indiana heard a case regarding burn injuries that involved a couple named McMahon who bought coffee from a mini-mart in a gas station. As they drove away, Mrs. McMahon started pouring the coffee into a smaller cup for her husband, who was driving. She later testified that the Styrofoam cup collapsed in her lap, leading to second- and third-degree burns from the coffee.

The couple sued the cup company for making a defective cup, and that case was settled out of court. They also sued the coffee machine maker (for making such hot coffee) and the seller (for keeping the coffee on a hot plate that maintained its high temperature). During the case against these defendants, Mr. McMahon said that when he bought the coffee, no warnings were placed on either the coffee maker or the decanter that kept it hot. The couple claimed they did not realize hot coffee could cause such severe burns and that coffee served hotter than 140 degrees is not fit for human consumption, making it "defective."

The parties had agreed to abide by a judge's decision (rather than a jury's). Ruling for the defendants, the judge noted that both McMahons testified they knew coffee was hot and that they had wanted to buy coffee that was hot. They admitted taking some precautions while handling and drinking coffee in the past, in order to prevent spills and burns. The judge said that as adult coffee drinkers who knew enough to be careful, they were not entitled to damages. The fact that the Styrofoam cup was defective did not render the coffee machine defective for serving a beverage meant to be served hot. Furthermore, coffee served between 175 and 185 degrees is within the normal range for the industry. The judge discussed the nature of coffee itself, saying that it must be brewed at a certain temperature for optimal taste and aroma. To ensure a drinking temperature of 150–160 degrees, coffee must be hotter in the pot, since it begins to cool as it is poured and prepared for drinking. The judge said in part that:

> [I]t is easy to sympathize with Angelina McMahon, severely injured by a common household beverage—and, for all we can see, without fault on her part. Using the legal system to shift the costs of this injury to someone else may be attractive to the McMahons, but it would have bad consequences for coffee fanciers who like their beverage hot. . . . First-party health and accident insurance deals with injuries of the kind Angelina suffered without the high costs of adjudication, and without potential side effects such as lukewarm coffee. . . . Indiana law does not make Bunn and similar firms insurers through the tort system of the harms, even grievous ones, that are common to the human existence.[2]

What Is Product Liability?

These two legal cases involve product liability—a type of personal injury law in which people claim a product caused an injury. When injuries or property damage occur from a product acquired through a commercial transaction (a sale or lease), the manufacturer may be liable if the product is defective or was misrepresented in terms of its safety or performance.

Each year, millions of people are injured, get sick, or die as a result of defective or dangerous products, such as motor vehicles, foods and beverages, pharmaceuticals, medical devices, personal care products, toys, household appliances, sports and exercise equipment, farm machinery, chemicals, and firearms. People who cannot resolve their grievances with the manufacturer may turn to the courts. Major court battles have ensued over tobacco products, motor vehicles, prescription drugs, medical devices, asbestos, and food products, among others.

Product liability cases are heard in civil, not criminal, courts. They come under an area of civil law called torts, from the French word meaning *wrong*. Torts occur when people suffer an injury because of the action or inaction of a party who has a duty to exercise due care. Most product liability cases are unintentional torts, meaning the defendants did not knowingly make or sell products intended to harm people.

Depending on the circumstances, a person might name one or more defendants: those who made or assembled the product; those who supplied any parts; testing laboratories; and/or those who distributed, sold, or repaired the product. Plaintiffs can ask for monetary damages, including compensatory damages for economic losses (e.g., lost income, medical costs, property damage, lost future earnings) and non-economic damages (e.g., pain and suffering, disability, disfigurement). They also may seek punitive damages, which are designed to punish and deter the behavior of the defendant.

Although estimates vary, hundreds of billions of dollars move through the U.S. legal system annually for cases involving product liability. These costs include payments from manufacturers and service providers (and their insurers) to plaintiffs and their attorneys, either in pre-trial settlements or after the case is heard in court. Costs also include legal fees paid to the defendants' attorneys. One study put the 2007 figure at more than $800 billion.[3]

Product cases may involve complex issues. Looking at the Liebeck case, author Philip K. Howard writes:

How do we prove whether hot coffee is unreasonable? Hotter coffee brews better and stays warmer longer. It can also scald. Hundreds of people had complained about McDonald's coffee over the years. But billions of cups—over one billion cups per year—kept being sold, indicating some measure of market acceptance. Why should a drive-thru window sell such hot coffee? Why not, aren't drivers grown up? Where do you draw the line? You can argue it either way.[4]

Laws governing product liability have developed over centuries. This process is called common law, case law, or judge-made law. The courts also must follow the laws passed by state legislatures. All 50 states have adopted—in full or in part—the Uniform Commercial Code (UCC), which is not a federal law but instead is the result of a nationwide effort to make laws affecting businesses similar from state to state. Courts in each state, however, might interpret laws differently, and the law of product liability continues to evolve as new cases arise.

A Brief History of Product Liability

Before the advent of the Industrial Revolution in the eighteenth century, many products people purchased were often grown or made locally and sold in face-to-face transactions between individuals who knew each other. Today, the manufacturing, production, shipment, and sale of most goods can involve many different people who never meet. Technology also exposes people to dangers that our ancestors never imagined.

Not surprisingly, people have been concerned about the quality of the goods they traded or bought since ancient times. The general attitude during some eras is expressed in the Latin phrase *caveat emptor*—meaning "let the buyer beware." Buyers were supposed to take care and even look for hidden defects in a product. This was obviously easier when goods were fairly simple in nature and people bought them straight from the seller.

Laws did develop to hold sellers responsible for fraud or for expressly warranting something that was false. By A.D. 533, Roman law put more responsibility on sellers for a basic implied (unspoken) warranty of quality. Sellers were responsible for their goods, to the extent that the goods contained no hidden defects that would make them unsuitable for the ordinary purpose for which they were sold. European countries gradually adopted the standard of implied warranty of quality. By the 1500s, it had become English common law, as set forth in various court opinions. This idea prevailed in colonial America, where English law formed the basis for many American laws.

Legal scholar Walton H. Hamilton has found that the phrase *caveat emptor* first appeared in legal literature in 1534, but it was not commonly used in British or American law cases until the 1800s.[5] Rather, from the 1400s through the 1700s, the law

THE LETTER OF THE LAW

Excerpt from the French Commercial Code of 1807 (following Roman law)

§ II. Of the Warranty against Defects in the Thing sold.

641. The seller is bound to warranty in respect of secret defects in the thing sold which render it improper for the use to which it is destined, or which so far diminish such use, that the buyer would not have purchased it, or would not have given so large a price, if he had known them.

642. The seller is not bound against apparent faults and such as the purchaser might have taken cognizance of himself.

643. He is bound against concealed faults, even though he was not aware of them, unless in such case it have been stipulated that he should not be bound to any warranty.

Source: French Civil Code, Book III, Chapter IV, Section III, http://www.napoleon-series.org/research/government/code/book3/c_title06.html#section3.

regarding the sale of goods reflected the idea of "a fair price, full measure, and good workmanship."[6]

Until the late 1800s, the buyer needed to have a contract with the seller to recover damages for injuries resulting from a product. The often-cited English case of *Winterbottom v. Wright* (1842) reaffirmed this narrower view of liability. Winterbottom, the driver of a stagecoach for the postmaster general, was injured after the coach broke down and turned over. Wright, the manufacturer, had supplied the coach and had contracted with the coach's owner to keep it in good repair. The judge, Lord Abinger, ruled in favor of the manufacturer, reasoning that the "victim of product accident could not maintain a negligence action against a seller without privity of contract." In other words, only the purchaser could sue the seller. Lord Abinger expressed concerns that numerous legal cases could arise if people could sue under these circumstances: "If the plaintiff can sue, every passenger or even any person passing along the road, who was injured by the upsetting of the coach, might bring a similar action. Unless we confine the operation of such contracts as this to the parties who enter into them, the most absurd and outrageous consequences, to which I can see no limit, would ensue."[7]

The law of product liability, however, evolved beyond the scope of contract law (based on the agreement of two or more parties) and into tort law (based on damage caused, regardless of the parties' relationship). The first English-language treatise on the subject, Francis Hilliard's *The Law of Torts, or Private Wrongs*, was published in 1859. As courts heard more personal injury cases involving products, they tried to balance the rights and responsibilities of the parties. Courts often were willing to favor plaintiffs if manufacturers had committed outright fraud or deception (e.g., selling medicines with known dangers).

The Industrial Revolution brought new challenges as goods were produced and sold on a massive scale. Improved methods of transportation meant that more strangers were transacting business in different states. Courts, however, still were unwilling to let people sue remote sellers with whom they had no contact, but sometimes exceptions were made to promote justice for injured persons. As legal historian Lawrence M. Friedman writes:

> Every legal system tries to redress harm done by one person to another. The industrial revolution added an appalling increase in dimension. Its machines produced injuries as well as profits and products. The profits were a tempting and logical fund out of which to pay the costs of the injured. Moreover, the industrial relationship was impersonal. No ties of blood or love prevented one cog in the machine from suing the machine and its owners. But precisely here (to the 19th-century mind) lay the danger. Lawsuits and damages might injure the health of precarious enterprise. The machines were the basis for economic growth, for national wealth, for the greater good of society.[8]

In addition to expanding the category of people who might sue for damages, tort law also evolved to allow compensation for a wider range of conduct. Courts began to allow plaintiffs to sue for negligence. Instead of looking for intentional harm, negligence law let the courts consider cases in which people accidentally sold a defective or dangerous product. These cases involved more diverse items, including foods, personal care products, and durable goods such as cars.

As plaintiffs gained ground, courts found ways to balance competing interests. When an accident seemed like an unavoidable part of life, the plaintiff was not likely to win. Debates raged over the "assumption of risk" and what constituted "truly unavoidable harm." These debates continue today. The legal theory of contributory negligence placed some responsibility on injured plaintiffs, rather than holding manufacturers strictly accountable. By showing that a plaintiff was even partially at fault, defendants could avoid paying damages.

In their own defense, manufacturers could say they used "ordinary care" in making their products. This standard was articulated in 1850 when the Massachusetts Supreme Court looked at whether the action was "willful, intentional, or careless" in the case of *Brown v. Kendall*. The court decided:

> In using this term, ordinary care, it may be proper to state that what constitutes ordinary care will vary with the circumstances of cases. In general, it means that kind and degree of care, which prudent and cautious men would use, such as required by the exigency of the case, and such as is necessary to guard against probable danger.

Chief Justice Shaw went on to say that when people did use "due care and all proper precautions," an accident could still result, but this would be *involuntary*, and *unavoidable*."[9]

Though this was not a product liability case, it influenced the way courts viewed the rights and duties of the parties in tort cases—courts could decide whether a manufacturer had exercised "due care/ordinary care" or not. Some judges, however, expressed concerns that juries tended to favor plaintiffs, even when these plaintiffs also had been negligent. In the 1852 case of *Haring v. New York and Erie Railroad Co.*, the judge commented that "compassion will sometimes exercise over the ... jury, an influence which, however honorable to them as philanthropists, is wholly inconsistent with the principles of law and the ends of justice."[10]

By the 1880s, courts were requiring more of manufacturers, including affirmative duties to protect consumers from harm. The courts moved toward stricter standards of liability by looking for ways the manufacturer could have made the product safer. As technology provided better designs and techniques, more accidents and injuries seemed preventable.

Along with that, courts considered whether the injury was foreseeable. In an 1882 case, a contractor who built a scaffold was found negligent when this scaffold broke, injuring a painter.

The court said the contractor could have foreseen that improper construction would be dangerous to anyone who would use the scaffold for the purpose for which it was constructed, so he owed these people a duty.[11] Courts also sided with the plaintiff when a defective coffee urn exploded in a restaurant kitchen. They said that this machine "was of such a character inherently that . . . it was liable to become a source of great danger to many people if not carefully and properly constructed."[12] In other cases, defendants were found liable for defects in the making of engines, elevators, farm equipment, and canned foods.

Modern Product Liability Law

A landmark 1916 case moved American courts closer to modern product liability law. Benjamin Cardozo, an influential New York judge who would later become a U.S. Supreme Court justice, wrote the majority opinion. Soon after purchasing a new Buick, Donald MacPherson was driving a sick neighbor to the hospital when the wooden spokes on his left rear wheel crumbled, causing the car to collapse. MacPherson was thrown from the car and injured after he was pinned under the axle. This wheel, which Buick had purchased from another company, was made from defective wood. As a defense, Buick claimed there was no privity of contract between their company and MacPherson because he bought the car from a dealer.

The New York court rejected that defense and ruled in MacPherson's favor, awarding him $5,000. The ruling was significant, for Buick neither had a direct contractual relationship with MacPherson nor exhibited any deliberate misconduct; the company simply failed to identify the defect through inspection. Though the automaker had bought the wheels from a reputable manufacturer, Cardozo said that Buick still had a duty to inspect them, because the company was responsible for the finished product. Buick should have used "ordinary and simple tests" on the parts before placing their product on the market, Cardozo noted. Furthermore, automakers should be liable not only with regard to the car owner but also to other persons who would use the car: "We think that injury to others is to be foreseen not merely as a possible, but as an almost inevitable result."[13]

Some of the judges on the case dissented from Cardozo's opinion. They thought Buick had fulfilled its legal duties and could not have foreseen the problem. Judge Willard Bartlett noted that Buick relied on the wheel company to provide a safe product and that it had furnished "eighty thousand wheels, none of which had proved to be made of defective wood prior to the accident in the present case."[14] He cited the *Winterbottom* case and quoted Lord Abinger's comment about the "absurd and out-rageous consequences" that may result if people can sue in these kinds of cases.

Other courts, however, adopted Cardozo's line of reasoning. Between 1916 and 1982, the so-called "MacPherson rule" was used in every state. Contract law no longer limited this area of the law, and under tort law, manufacturers had more duties to take care in the ways they designed, inspected, and fabricated products.

FROM THE BENCH

MacPherson v. Buick Motor Co., 217 N.Y. 382, 111 N.E. 1050 (1916)

In the influential New York Court of Appeals opinion that removed privity of contract from negligence lawsuits, Judge Benjamin Cardozo wrote:

> There is evidence . . . that its defects could have been discovered by reasonable inspection, and that an inspection was omitted. There is no claim that the defendant knew of the defect and willfully concealed it. . . . The charge is one, not of fraud, but of negligence. . . . If the nature of a thing is such that it is reasonably certain to place life and limb in peril when negligently made, it is then a thing of danger.

Source: *MacPherson v. Buick Motor Co.*, 217 N.Y. 382, 111 N.E. 1050 (1916), http://www.lawrence.edu/fast/boardmaw/MacPhrsn_Bu.html.

This February 1932 photo shows Judge Benjamin Cardozo on his last day in the New York Court of Appeals before going on to the U.S. Supreme Court. In an influential 1916 New York Court of Appeals opinion, Cardozo helped to form the basis for modern product liability law.

Cardozo issued other rulings that affected product liability. In *Adams v. Bullock* (1919), Cardozo's court looked at the costs of preventing even the remotest possibility of injury. It concluded that companies did not have a duty to protect against any possible occurrence when the probability of an accident was low and the cost of preventing it was high. In his decision, Cardozo did mention a "duty to adopt all reasonable precautions." This decision set the stage for an approach in which courts weighed the risk of harm, the gravity of that harm, and the overall costs of preventing it.[15] Such an approach is today called a "cost-benefit analysis."

Courts continued to expand ways in which plaintiffs could recover damages. In a 1932 case, a man was injured when his car windshield shattered during an accident. He did not have a contract with the carmaker but brought a lawsuit based on fraud. There was an express warranty that said the windshield was shatterproof, but this was untrue. The court agreed that a consumer should have a strict liability cause of action, with no need to show negligence or privity, when a seller represented its products as possessing "qualities which they, in fact, do not possess" and the customer suffers damages as a result.[16]

In 1944, the California Supreme Court made a landmark decision in product liability. A waitress named Gladys Escola was putting away bottles of Coca-Cola when one of them exploded, causing a deep cut that severed blood vessels and nerves in her hand. At the trial, a company deliveryman testified that he had seen other bottles of the beverage explode spontaneously. This case was decided on the basis of *res ipsa loquitur*—from Latin words meaning "the thing speaks for itself." The court concluded that the bottle was defective when it arrived at the restaurant and that Escola was harmed as a direct result of that defect. The court found Coca-Cola negligent, but the concurring opinion by Justice Roger J. Traynor went even further:

> I concur in the judgment, but I believe the manufacturer's negligence should no longer be singled out as the basis of a plaintiff's right to recover in cases like the present one. In my opinion it should now be recognized that a manufacturer incurs an absolute liability when an article that he has placed on the market, knowing that it is to be used without inspection, proves to have a defect that causes injury to human beings. . . . Even if there is no negligence . . . public policy demands that responsibility be fixed wherever it will most effectively reduce the hazards to life and health inherent in defective products that reach the market.[17]

Traynor's reasoning spurred courts to assign more responsibility to manufacturers under a theory of strict product liability, meaning liability without fault, negligence, or privity of contract. In the pivotal 1960 case *Henningsen v. Bloomfield Motors, Inc.*, a court applied a strict liability standard when a defective automobile caused injuries. The Supreme Court of California also applied strict liability in the landmark 1963 case *Greenman v. Yuba Power Products, Inc.* Writing for a unanimous court, Justice Traynor wrote:

> Manufacturers of defective products are strictly liable in tort to persons injured by such products, irrespective of any contract limitations that might inhere in the law of warranty. . . . The purpose of such liability is to insure that the costs of injuries resulting from defective products are borne by the manufacturers [and sellers] that put such products on the market rather than by the injured persons who are powerless to protect themselves.[18]

This put the focus on the condition of the product, not on the seller's conduct.

The American Law Institute (ALI) adopted this doctrine in the Restatement (Second) of Torts of 1965. The Restatement reflects the thinking of legal scholars regarding tort law, and the courts generally use this reasoning when deciding cases. Of course, even when referring to the same restatement, courts do interpret the material differently.

Strict product liability expanded plaintiffs' rights and gave defendants fewer defenses. Manufacturers had a duty to design and make products that were safe under more diverse conditions. For example, car companies were expected to design the car so as to protect people during a crash, even though cars were not produced with the thought of crashing in mind.[19] Courts also expanded the idea of "reasonably anticipated use" to include more kinds of misuse by consumers, if the manufacturers could "reasonably foresee" such misuse. In a 1969 case, the Missouri Supreme Court said that plaintiffs could recover under strict liability unless they had put the product to an abnormal use, did not use the product in a manner reasonably anticipated, or did not use it in a way it was intended to be used.[20]

As the duty to warn became more rigorous, product labels came under closer scrutiny. Cases involving warning labels also looked at ways people might misuse a product and considered whether such misuse was "foreseeable." In 1982, the New Jersey Supreme Court even held that a product was defective "for not bearing a warning against an unforeseeable risk."[21] Critics have called that decision unfair and illogical. This court did modify this decision two years later, saying, "Manufacturers must only warn of risks they reasonably can foresee at the time they sell the product."[22] Cases involving warning labels continue to be controversial.

With strict liability in place, product liability cases increased. From 1974 to 1986, the number of cases in federal court rose from 1,500 to 13,500.[23] Cases involving personal injury increased six-fold from 1975 to 1989.[24]

Reform Efforts

By the late 1970s, critics were calling for major reforms in product liability, believing the laws were unfair and excessively costly for businesses—and therefore costly for the public, since these costs led manufacturers to set higher prices. Product liability insurance premiums tripled from 1984 to 1986.[25] During the 1980s, studies showed that about half of all awards and settlements went to attorneys and insurers for administering the settlement process—far higher than the administrative costs for the workers' compensation system (30 percent) and the Social Security system (1 percent).[26] Critics also complained that the system was unpredictable because of diverse laws around the country.

To address such concerns, the U.S. Department of Commerce introduced its Model Uniform Product Liability Act (MUPLA) in 1979 and encouraged the states to adopt it, but various states adopted only parts of the act. States did consider their own reforms. According to the American Tort Reform Association (ATRA), from 1986 to 1990, 20 states enacted one or more laws to reform product liability.[27] Most of these changes tended to help businesses—for example, they set a standard of "foreseeable and reasonable" risk in regard to labels.

During the 1980s, various federal bills were considered and rejected. President Ronald Reagan lent his support when the U.S. House Committee on Energy and Commerce Subcommittee on Commerce, Consumer Protection and Competitiveness pushed its 1988 federal product liability bill (H.R. 1115), but it was defeated.

In 1993, another attempt to establish uniform product liability standards failed when Congress did not pass the Fairness in Product Liability Act. Congress did, however, pass acts to address specific areas of product liability involving vaccines, aviation, and medical devices. The Biomaterials Access Assurance Act of 1998 is one example. It provides immunity for the suppliers of materials used to make medical implants. Congress became concerned that companies would stop supplying materials to implant manufacturers because they feared being named in lawsuits if an implant proved to be defective.

QUOTABLE

President Bill Clinton, Statement on Signing the Biomaterials Access Assurance Act of 1998

The bill protects certain raw materials and parts suppliers from liability for harm caused by a medical implant. . . . Without those materials, Americans would have to live without the heart valves, jaw implants, artificial hips, and other medical devices (including many not yet imagined) that can help the victims of disease and injury stay alive or improve the quality of their lives.

Source: Administration of William J. Clinton, 1998, http://www.gpo.gov/fdsys/pkg/ WCPD-1998-08-17/pdf/WCPD-1998-08-17-Pg1623.pdf.

In 1997, the ALI put various reforms and clarifications into the Restatement (Third) of Torts. This restatement still applies strict liability to manufacturing defects, but design and warning defects are defined more in terms of negligence. Instead of talking about negligence, warranty, or strict tort liability, the ALI proposed using a functional products liability analysis, whether plaintiffs allege a manufacturing defect, design defect, or defect by reason of inadequate warnings or instructions. This restatement remains in place.

Today's Controversies

Major debates over product liability laws concern standards of liability, which critics consider unclear and too variable, and the kinds of tests and evidence that are used to decide whether products are defective. Other debates involve defenses to liability suits; statutes of limitations; the amounts of damage awards; and the roles of federal laws, state laws, and the courts.

Reformers grew more vocal during the 1990s as attorneys brought class-action lawsuits in the form of "mass tort" cases involving tobacco, asbestos, and other products that harmed many people over long periods of time. According to critics, these suits subjected companies to unfair statutes of limitation, double jeopardy, and an unending series of lawsuits, as well as excessive damages. To address these concerns, the Class Action Fairness Act of 2005, one of the few federal laws addressing product liability, was passed and signed into law by President George W. Bush.

Plaintiffs in a product liability case use various legal arguments and expert testimony to convince the court that a product is unreasonably dangerous or defective. The legal doctrine of *res ipsa loquitur* (the thing speaks for itself) shifts the burden of proof to the defendant to prove its company/business is not negligent. Under strict liability, the plaintiff need not prove negligence, only some kind of defect in the product. This allows people to recover damages without proving fault. If the product is not inherently dangerous; defective; or unfit in terms of negligence, implied

warranty, or strict liability, plaintiffs can claim it is more dangerous than it should be. Expert testimony explains how the danger
is excessive, how the defect could be prevented, and how the supposed defect led to a plaintiff's injuries. Plaintiffs try to convince
the court that the product carries a foreseeable risk that the users
should not have to bear, either because they cannot reasonably
expect such risks or because manufacturers have a reasonable
way to avoid them.

What makes something "defective" under the law? Courts
have found products defective in the way they are made and
assembled. Design problems would be present from the outset,
before the product was made, so it could be inherently unsafe.
Manufacturing defects can occur when products are made in such
a way that they do not meet the specifications of the designer
or manufacturer. This can occur accidentally or from unknown
causes during the assembly process and during quality checks.
Cases like these are easier to prove when a product is so dangerous
it should never have been on the market at all. Packaging defects
also can occur. Even if a product has been tampered with after it
was manufactured, the company still could be held liable for not
meeting a duty to provide tamper-proof packaging.

Defects in marketing are also cited, including improper
labeling, inadequate instructions, and insufficient safety warnings. Plaintiffs can try to prove negligence or use a strict liability
approach and say a reasonable alternative was available, and
courts are left to decide which side should prevail. Labeling and
warnings become especially important with products such as
chemicals, knives, and guns, which are hazardous by nature, yet
cannot be useful without also posing dangers. Proper warnings
about the dangers and risks of such products help users to make
informed decisions about using them, say advocates of strict
labeling standards. Cases over the duty to warn can become controversial, depending on how courts interpret that duty.

How do people defend themselves in these cases? The defendant seeks to prove the product was not defective, but that it was

instead properly manufactured and marketed. The issue of fault also comes into play, as defendants try to prove that a plaintiff was solely or partially responsible for the injuries or other problems that occurred. This is called contributory negligence. The plaintiffs might not have followed instructions or exercised reasonable care in using the product. Maybe they used it for an unintended purpose. They might have ignored warnings or agreed to use a product after being fully informed of the dangers. Perhaps they also ignored generally known dangers. If a plaintiff made changes to a product, such as removing safety features, the defendant can claim that this intervening event caused the injury to occur.

A defendant might also claim that something other than the product caused the harm, as tort law requires showing that the defendant caused the plaintiff's harm. With certain health problems, however, proving the cause can be difficult. For example, in asbestos cases, people have claimed their exposure to this substance caused certain health problems, but the plaintiffs might have developed these problems in other ways, such as from smoking for long periods of time. Some defendants have used a federal preemption defense, claiming manufacturers cannot be held responsible if they have complied with federal safety standards and have received approval from a federal agency. Some of these cases have reached the U.S. Supreme Court.

Critics call the current system slow, unpredictable, expensive, and inequitable. They say it encourages weak lawsuits, because courts have gone from looking at reasonable precautions in light of the probability of harm to holding defendants responsible for even the most remote chance of harm. Careful manufacturers also must imagine all sorts of misuses or lack of awareness on the part of consumers. Liability is so open-ended that people think someone should pay for any kind of accident or bad luck, even if they themselves were careless. Courts do not pay enough attention to assumption of risk and contributory negligence on the part of plaintiffs. As David G. Owen and Jerry

J. Phillips write, "To what extent is a manufacturer of a product responsible for the conduct, misconduct, forgetfulness, laziness, or downright stupidity of the user?"[28]

Punitive damages also have come under fire because critics say they often reflect jury members' negative feelings toward businesses and their desire to punish far beyond the actual harm the defendant's conduct caused. Reformers also have criticized lawyers for bringing cases they consider "frivolous" simply to earn large fees, especially when clients in large class-action suits receive smaller amounts.

Summary

Product liability law involves civil claims based on the idea that a product caused an injury. People who sue for damages in such cases use theories of negligence, breach of one or more warranties, strict product liability, and misrepresentation. They can claim defects in design and/or manufacture, as well as problems with warnings and/or instructions. Critics complain that the rise in litigation and large jury awards harm American businesses and make them less competitive globally. Supporters of the current system say strict accountability is needed to protect consumers' rights and to ensure safe products.

Questions have arisen over whether courts, state legislatures, or the federal government should make liability laws. Should federal product liability laws guide local courts? How much state diversity is acceptable in this area of the law? Who should bear the cost when injury/harm occurs? What standards of liability should be used, and what kinds of defenses can companies and manufacturers raise when they are sued? How can the law fairly balance the interests of the various parties? What awards for damages are reasonable versus excessive? Should judges or juries make the decisions in these cases? The following chapters look at different sides of these and other issues.

Federal Liability Laws Are Needed

The distinguished legal scholar Justice Oliver Wendell Holmes Jr. once described the law as "the prophecies of what the courts will do."[1] He wrote, "People want to know under what circumstances and how far they will run the risk of coming against what is so much stronger than themselves, and hence it becomes a business to find out when this danger is to be feared."[2]

This is not always possible in the area of product liability. Because laws vary across the country, businesses cannot always predict how or why courts will find them liable for injuries, how long after selling a product they might be liable, or what damages they will have to pay. Manufacturers have been found liable when they made state-of-the-art products or surpassed federal safety standards. Some laws hold them responsible for all damages even when the plaintiff was negligent and another party or parties contributed to the injury. Plaintiffs have won cases when they made changes in the product that caused it to be less safe.[3] They even have won when they did things the warning label told them not to do.

For these and other reasons, the nation needs uniform federal product liability legislation. Congress has attempted to pass such a bill for more than 30 years. In 1979, the Federal Interagency Task Force on Product Liability, appointed by President Jimmy Carter, produced its Model Uniform Product Liability Act. When few states adopted the act, Congress continued to discuss the need for uniform legal standards and procedures in product liability. Supporters of uniform standards proposed bills that addressed serious concerns. The Senate Committee that worked on a comprehensive 1997 reform bill noted that "the current morass of product liability laws is a problem of national concern that requires Congressional action."[4] Senator John McCain, the chairman of the Senate Committee on Commerce, Science, and Transportation at that time, endorsed the bill, and a majority of legislators agreed. Despite opposition from the trial attorneys' lobby and from others, this bill passed in both the U.S. House of Representatives and the Senate, but President Bill Clinton vetoed it. Since then, various federal laws have tried to reform specific areas that were addressed in that bill. States also have passed laws that reform one or more areas of product liability.

The current system is complex, inefficient, and unpredictable.

A uniform approach to product liability could improve efficiency and guarantee that more of the court-awarded damages reach the injured parties. Such uniformity also could improve fairness and ensure that people with similar complaints receive similar treatment from one court to another.

The nation's complex patchwork of laws causes problems for manufacturers, sellers, and injured persons alike. Laws, based on court decisions and various state and federal statutes, vary in terms of how they interpret liability and how much they hold each party liable for problems resulting from the use of a product. As previously mentioned, different courts may reach different results as they decide whether a product is defective. States also award damages differently, and companies may face multiple punitive damages awards from one state to another.

Similar and even identical cases can have very different results. This can happen even within one state when local courts have choices about how to apply the law. One court might dismiss a product liability case; in another court the case will proceed to trial. A person might sue a pharmaceutical company, alleging harm from a medication, and have the case dismissed, while someone in another state with the same grievance is permitted to sue. Some victims receive large monetary awards; others receive little to nothing.

Results often depend on the skills of the attorneys, as well as the juries themselves. Juries can reach different conclusions even with similar cases and legal issues. As one legal analyst notes, juries can disagree when they consider "the usefulness and desirability of the product, the likelihood that the product will cause injury, the availability of a substitute product that will meet the same need and not be as unsafe, and the producer's ability to eliminate the unsafe character of the product without impairing its usefulness or making it too expensive."[5]

Businesses often are surprised by court decisions. For instance, in 1985, a Pennsylvania court barred a company from using the defense that the design alternative that would have prevented the accident in question was not scientifically known at the time of the accident.[6] In *The Collapse of the Common Good*, Philip K. Howard describes two cases involving GM vehicles: In 1993, the company was found liable for $105.2 million when a pickup exploded after it was hit on the side. The plaintiffs argued that this explosion could have been averted if the tank had been placed elsewhere. In 1999, GM was found liable for $4.9 billion after a Chevrolet was hit from behind by a car traveling at high speed, and it exploded. In that case, the gas tank was located in the rear, and the plaintiffs said the explosion might not have occurred if the tank had been placed elsewhere. Howard asks, "Where is a manufacturer supposed to put the tank?"[7]

Other problems arise when people try to reconcile state and federal laws. In some cases, companies can comply with every federal regulation and receive federal approval but still lose in court. Cases often move along slowly as each side submits motions asking the court to apply different state or federal laws that would favor their cause.

Statutes of repose also vary, bringing even more uncertainty to the process. These statutes specify the amount of time a person has to sue after a product was manufactured. In 1985, a company was held liable for an injury that occurred when the plaintiff was using a printing press made in the 1890s. The machine had been modified quite a bit since then, and it was being used in a manner different from how it was originally intended. Nonetheless, a jury found that the Harris Corporation should pay the injured plaintiff $687,000.[8]

Manufacturers should not be held accountable for problems that occur when old products are used beyond their normal lifespan. They should not be liable indefinitely, either. Yet, as of 2006, only 19 states have a statute of repose.[9] Europe has set consistent standards so that a company cannot be sued in regard to products older than 10 years. A federal standard in the United States could set a specific and reasonable amount of time.

In the absence of a uniform law, states have passed their own statutes of repose and statues of limitation for filing product liability suits. Illinois, for example, set a 12-year limit. In 2000, the Oregon Law Commission noted, "While many jurisdictions have enacted specific time limitations for product liability actions, differences among the statutes far outnumber the similarities leaving no discernable trend."[10]

The unpredictable nature of product liability has serious consequences. Businesses may be forced to defend lawsuits in different ways in different courts if the product in question is mass-produced and marketed throughout the country. This requires extra time and money that will be taken from the businesses, and these costs will be passed on to consumers. Companies find it difficult to plan their activities and to determine how much insurance coverage they will need year to year. Insurance companies also need some consistency and predictability. A spokesperson for the Alliance of American Insurers said, "If insurance is to work, insurers must be able to predict how frequently insured events will take place, and how large a loss those events are likely to cause. Predictability in these elements is essential for insurers to price their coverage and to know the extent of the liability they are assuming under the insurance contract."[11] Author Michael Ena points out, "While the certainty, predictability, and uniformity of results are generally less important in tort cases, in the products liability context, predictability of judicial decisions is an important factor in evaluating business risks associated with the marketing of a particular product."[12]

Injured plaintiffs also fare differently from court to court, and recent cases show how inequitable these results can be. In a 1999 case in Oregon, a man who suffered from partial paralysis, severe brain damage, and disability when a nail gun misfired additional nails received only $475,000 in noneconomic damages.[13] That same year, a court in another state awarded $80 million in noneconomic damages to the widow of a man who died of lung cancer after smoking for 42 years.[14]

Congress and federal agencies can develop better standards than courts and state legislatures.

Under the current system, lawyers, local judges, and juries can make laws instead of leaving lawmaking to elected officials who are accountable to the public. Courtroom decisions can have far-reaching effects on public policy, yet laws shaped by judges and lawyers do not go through the democratic process. Critics have said that this raises constitutional issues. In 2002, Professor

Stephen B. Presser wrote, "American courts have—over the last thirty years—usurped the law-making function of American legislatures."[15]

Statistics show that local judges and juries are inclined to view situations in ways that favor local plaintiffs over distant defendants, especially when the plaintiff has effective attorneys. Local courts have more incentives to help local citizens at the expense of companies, most of them out-of-state, especially when the juries perceive these companies as having "deep pockets." Elected judges know that their decisions can affect their chances of being reelected. In his book *The Product Liability Mess*, Judge Richard Neely, former chief justice of the West Virginia Supreme Court, points out that individual states are unlikely to take a leading role in reforming the system, since liberal laws that allow plaintiffs to prevail can benefit the courts' home states in various ways.[16]

Elected officials in Washington are better suited to determine which policies will benefit the nation as a whole because they are more likely to strike a balance among competing interests and can debate the complex social, scientific, and economic issues at hand. Members of Congress also are more inclined to consider both the costs and benefits of various policies. Their final vote will reflect the thinking of a larger, more diverse, and better-informed group than the typical jury or local court.

Congress already has seen the need to take action in regards to specific products. During the 1970s and 1980s, juries across the nation awarded large sums of money to people who claimed they were injured from vaccines, either because of inadequate warnings, side effects, or problems that occurred during manufacturing. State courts upheld these judgments. By 1986, the vaccine industry was so vulnerable to excessive liability that public health officials feared they might stop developing and making vaccines. Prices rose as manufacturers paid more for insurance. Vaccination had reduced the incidence of and death rate due to once-epidemic diseases, including smallpox, polio, measles, and whooping cough (pertussis). A small percentage of vaccine recipients, however, are seriously harmed. Experts said the risks, though obviously severe for the individuals who are hurt, were relatively small compared to the benefits for millions of people.

Congress balanced these interests with a law that protects vaccine makers and sets up a fund and compensation process for rightful victims. To collect, people need not prove negligence. Decisions are based on a Vaccine Injury Table, which was developed by scientific experts who reviewed the studies and literature on vaccines to identify what kinds of adverse reactions can reasonably be attributed to vaccines. Funding comes from a combination of federal taxes and an excise tax on each dose of vaccine.

Likewise, Congress saw that diverse liability laws relating to medical devices were stifling innovation, whereas a uniform standard could encourage research and development. For that reason, Congress passed the Medical Devices Amendment to the Food and Drug Act. In the 2008 case *Riegel v. Medtronic, Inc.*, the U.S. Supreme Court upheld this federal preemption.[17]

Other Congressional acts work in the public interest to balance the needs involved. The General Aviation Revitalization Act of 1994 set an 18-year statute of repose in this area of torts to revive the private aircraft industry. Examples of other effective federal product laws include the Biomaterials Access Assurance Act of 1998, the Multiparty, Multiforum Trial Jurisdiction Act of 2002, and the Protection of Lawful Commerce in Arms Act of 2003.

Opponents claim national standards jeopardize product safety, but this seems unlikely, as federal regulatory agencies are well positioned to address safety concerns. Analysts have said that federal laws and regulations through agencies like the National Highway Traffic Safety Administration (NHTSA) have played a key role in reducing accident rates.

Experts who have access to less biased information can evaluate the evidence and weigh risks and benefits more wisely than juries. In tort cases, juries look at events that already occurred. Risks may be easier to detect in hindsight. Lawmakers can make sure that regulations focus on the primary goals of product liability law—to minimize risks, to promote safe products, and to compensate victims of product-related injuries. Through discussion and debate, using the input of impartial experts, lawmakers can arrive at a more reasonable social risk policy than the current fragmented product liability system provides.

Uniform standards for warnings could improve consumer safety. W. Kip Viscusi and Alan Schwartz recommend what Viscusi called "a national warnings policy to establish a uniform national vocabulary for warnings."[18] Scientific studies can provide the basis for developing sound, effective warnings. As Viscusi said, this approach would "establish objective criteria to serve as a reference point for assessing warnings" instead of having so-called warning label experts arguing in court.[19] Using a common language and warnings format also would help individuals read and understand warnings more easily. Viscusi noted, "The best method of achieving a well-designed warnings system is not to let the warnings system emerge from a series of decentralized court cases."[20]

A uniform federal standard would benefit the U.S. economy.

The present product liability system impacts interstate commerce and global business transactions. The Commerce Clause to the U.S. Constitution gives Congress the power to intervene when necessary in order to regulate commerce. In ratifying this amendment, the nation's founders intended to limit each state in what it can do to bring more fairness, predictability, and consistency to product liability law. This means the federal government must step in.

Clause 18 of Section 8, known as the "Necessary and Proper Clause" of the Constitution, supports this power. It states that the Commerce Clause and all of the other enumerated powers may be implemented by the power vested in Congress. In 1997, the Senate Committee took note of the impact on interstate commerce when it wrote these sections of the federal product liability reform bill:

> (2) excessive, unpredictable, and often arbitrary damage awards and unfair allocations of liability have a direct and undesirable effect on interstate commerce by increasing the cost and decreasing the availability of goods and services....

> (8) because of the national scope of the problems created by the defects in the civil justice system, it is not possible for the States to enact laws that fully and effectively respond to those problems;

THE LETTER OF THE LAW

Excerpts from the United States Constitution

Article I, Section 1

All legislative Powers herein granted shall be vested in a Congress of the United States, which shall consist of a Senate and House of Representatives....

Article I, Section 8, Clause 3

The Congress shall have Power ... To regulate Commerce with foreign Nations, and among the several States, and with the Indian Tribes....

Article I, Section 8, Clause 18

To make all Laws which shall be necessary and proper for carrying into Execution the foregoing Powers, and all other Powers vested by this Constitution in the Government of the United States, or in any Department or Officer thereof.

Source: http://www.senate.gov/civics/constitution_item/constitution.htm

(9) it is the constitutional role of the national government to remove barriers to interstate commerce and to protect due process rights.[21]

Clear, consistent standards would encourage more business activity, including innovation. Companies are more likely to introduce new products if they have a clearer idea about how different state laws will affect their commercial activities. As one businessman told Congress during hearings on product liability reform, "We need new products in America. We need updated products. We need the leading technology. We believe we have to sit back and say we better not do this; we better not bring this product forward because we don't know what the rules are."[22]

A group of researchers found that product liability had, for example, led companies to stop developing new contraceptives. They found that a major factor was "the unpredictable nature of litigation, which results in part from the absence of stable and uniform national products liability rules and in part from the often erratic nature of the litigation system." They also noted, "Although manufacturers may introduce evidence of compliance with FDA regulations in a contraceptive products liability lawsuit, this evidence is given no special status in most states, such as entitling the manufacturer to a presumption that it acted with due care."[23]

Product liability affects global competitiveness. According to Professor Stephen B. Presser, European manufacturers "operate in a more predictable, less costly and less litigious legal environment."[24] Presser lists features in the European system that prevent excess litigation, including lower damage judgments, absence of punitive damages, non-use of juries in civil cases, and the absence of contingent fees for attorneys. He notes that European countries have used legislation rather than the courts to reform social policies and to improve consumer protection. It makes sense to harmonize the American civil justice system with the European model, says Presser, "if American manufacturers are going to be able to compete effectively in the global market-place and if American consumers are going to continue to enjoy the benefits of technological innovation."[25]

A uniform law could reduce problems associated with forum shopping.

In product cases, parties to a legal proceeding have what is called a "choice of law," in terms of where the case will be heard. A choice of courts is possible because products might be made in one or more states and purchased in another state, while the company and injured person might reside in still other states. At least 70 percent of all goods manufactured in a given state are shipped to at least one other state.[26] Attorneys obviously prefer to file their cases in the most favorable place for their client(s)—a practice known as forum shopping. Inequitable results can occur for both plaintiffs and defendants. Certain places have become known as "magnet jurisdictions," because of their high rate of favorable decisions and huge damage awards for plaintiffs.

Forum shopping means that parties with only a marginal connection to a case (e.g., a store that sold the product) might be named in the suit if they live or operate in one of the "favorable" jurisdictions. Plaintiffs can seek ways to have their case heard in a place with a more generous statute of limitations or statute of repose if the plaintiff lives in a state where these have expired. This situation became especially complicated in mass tort cases in which large numbers of people claimed they were injured because of long-term exposure to a substance, such as asbestos. Plaintiffs in some of those cases said they were exposed to asbestos made by several companies located in different states.

The federal government addressed this problem with the Class Action Fairness Act of 2005. In class action suits where plaintiffs are asking for at least $5 million in damages, it is possible to have the case heard in federal court rather than in a state court. Laws like this, however, are only a start. A more

comprehensive unified approach is needed to resolve the ongo-
ing problems in product liability law.

Summary

The current system—without uniform federal liability laws—can
result in widely different decisions across the country, even when
cases are similar. A comprehensive federal law could ensure
that injured parties are fairly compensated while also protecting businesses from extreme penalties and frivolous litigation.
It would bring much-needed stability to the current fragmented
system. Support for such a law has come from the United
States Small Business Administration, the National Association of
Manufacturers, the National Federation of Independent Business,
insurance companies, and numerous legal experts. Author E.
Patrick McGuire quotes one executive who said, "We can live
with nearly any system as long as there are some standard rules
or guidelines. We may not like the system, but at least we can plan
for it."[27]

Federal Liability Laws Are Unnecessary

Should the United States adopt a "one size fits all" approach to product liability? Consumer groups, organizations of attorneys, and groups that support states' rights are among those who oppose such centralized decision making. The current system recognizes the nation's strong federalist traditions and provides for a separation of powers between branches of government, which allows for progress and adjustments as case law evolves throughout the country. Other important benefits of the current system include flexibility, more fairness for injured individuals, and greater product safety for consumers.

A uniform law gives too much power to the federal government.

The United States' tradition of federalism provides for states' rights, with certain powers granted to the president, to Congress, and to the federal courts, with the remainder reserved for the states. This model keeps the federal government from assuming too much power in the affairs of states, including in their court system and in their local governments. Congress lacks the authority to interfere in an area the Constitution reserves for the states—in this case, tort law. On these grounds, the U.S. Conference of Chief Justices, the state governors, and the National Association of Attorneys General have criticized proposals to standardize all product liability laws. The Supreme Court has supported this separation of powers in numerous decisions. Such a law also has no precedent, because it would force all the state courts to abide by a federal statute and would only allow access to federal courts in cases where parties to the lawsuit lived in different states.

To justify such a bill, supporters say Congress has the right to govern in areas that involve interstate commerce, based on the Commerce Clause of the Constitution. They disregard the fact that the Commerce Clause traditionally has been used in cases in which states were erecting barriers to interstate commerce as a way to promote their own interests.

The U.S. Supreme Court also has challenged this line of reasoning. In *United States v. Lopez*, the Court said that Congress incurs "a very heavy burden when affecting areas of traditional state concern."[1] This was not a product liability case but did involve the subject of interstate commerce. Congress claimed that the Commerce Clause gave it the power to pass a law that banned guns in and around public schools throughout America. The Court disagreed. Chief Justice William H. Rehnquist wrote that Congress was limited in how it could apply this clause to various matters involving the states.[2] To show the intent of those who wrote the Constitution, Rehnquist quoted James Madison, who wrote, "The powers delegated by the proposed Constitution to the federal government are few and defined. Those which are to remain in the State governments are numerous and indefinite."[3]

The Court clearly meant to protect the states' right to use their own police power and legal system to bring people to justice. Making and selling products that can cause harm does not fall under the meaning of rightful commercial transactions. In this and other cases, the Supreme Court has reiterated that the Constitution not only permits but also supports the rights of states to develop diverse legal approaches. In *State Farm Mutual Auto Ins. Co. v. Campbell*, the Court noted that federalism means "each State may make its own reasoned judgment about what conduct is permitted or proscribed within its borders."[4]

Federal regulations already affect too many areas of product liability. In recent decades, Congress has enacted the National Childhood Vaccine Injury Act of 1986, the General Aviation Revitalization Act of 1994, the Biomaterials Access Assurance Act of 1998, the Multiparty, Multiforum Trial Jurisdiction Act of 2002, and the Protection of Lawful Commerce in Arms Act of 2003. These measures attempt to address so-called problems with product liability law but can go too far. Various federal bills that preempt state laws often have been adopted based on unproven claims that the current system is somehow inadequate or dysfunctional.

Principles of federalism recognize the importance of democracy at the local and state level. They acknowledge that local lawmakers need to consider geographical, economic, and community standards when they make decisions. Local community standards can be sensibly applied to cases involving personal injuries. Government officials in Washington do not understand these local concerns or the regional differences that justify different approaches.

Furthermore, the Seventh Amendment to the Constitution affirms the right to a trial by jury. Courts have pointed to this amendment when striking down state laws that attempt to change procedures for tort lawsuits or that limit the damages people can recover for their injuries.

Advocates of a uniform federal standard claim that local courts favor plaintiffs and say juries are too emotional and uninformed to make fair, balanced decisions. Statistics dispute that conclusion. In fact, some studies show that judges are more likely than juries to rule in favor of the plaintiff. The U.S. Department of Justice, Bureau of Justice Statistics Report for 1996 showed that judges ruled for plaintiffs in 57 percent of the cases, as compared to 48 percent for juries.[5]

Even within a state's borders, problems can occur when legislators assume too much power over the courts. In Ohio, for example, the legislature tried to change the rules applying to evidence and judicial procedure in tort cases. The state constitution assigns that role exclusively to the Ohio Supreme Court, which struck down this legislation. In Illinois, the state's supreme court struck down a tort law passed by the state legislature on the grounds that "the legislature is prohibited from enacting laws that unduly infringe upon the inherent powers of judges."[6] Numerous court challenges would likely take place if Congress passed a federal law that aimed to replace state laws or put too many restrictions on juries.

The different branches of government can cooperate, and courts can respect recommendations from the U.S. Congress,

QUOTABLE

David Walsh

The civil jury system has stood the test of time. It is a vibrant form of democratic accountability.... The system determines or apportions responsibility, compensates the wrongly injured and encourages safe behavior and accountability, such as the manufacture of safe products and delivery of non-negligent services.

Source: David Walsh, "Tort Reform: Necessity or Myth?" Wisconsin Business Alumni Update, June 2005, http://www.bus.wisc.edu/update/june05/tortreform.asp.

but federal legislation should not replace case law and state laws with one sweeping federal law. As Robert S. Peck writes, "What tort restrictionists want is nothing less than the elevation of the designs of today's transient legislature over the words and intent of those who framed each state's organic law."[7]

Replacing centuries of well-founded case law would be disruptive and confusing.

A uniform federal law would arbitrarily replace duly developed laws in all 50 states with one rigid standard. During hearings for a federal product liability bill in 1984, Howell Heflin, a Democratic senator who once served on the Alabama Supreme Court, pointed out the drawbacks of this kind of legislation. Heflin noted that such a law "would destroy the body of product liability law that the states have carefully developed to compensate victims of unsafe products and would permanently disrupt the common law process which produced that body of law."[8]

Changing to a single federal standard runs counter to legal traditions that have operated since the founding of the nation. For more than 200 years, courts with local judges and juries have shaped product liability laws, and courts and state legislators throughout the country have shared in their development. The results reflect the unique history and values of the individual states. States that see a problem in the laws have made adjustments both in their legislatures and in their courts to balance the interests of parties in product liability suits.

Such changes to the current system are not only undesirable but also unnecessary. Reformers point to a crisis in product liability litigation, but recent statistics show that the number of cases has been declining. The number of product cases in federal courts reached a high of 28,000 in 2004, but that number declined by 14 percent the next year. The decline continued in 2005 and 2006.[9]

Switching to a uniform standard could result in greater confusion instead of greater clarity. Through the years, a mix of federal, state, and common law has emerged in the various federal reform bills. Such a mix can make it difficult, not easier, to reach decisions. Numerous difficulties could arise as state courts try to interpret the provisions in the new law and then apply the law within the context of their own state laws. People likely would file lawsuits to protest changes in previously settled areas of the law, and the U.S. Supreme Court would be swamped with complaints involving constitutional issues.

Moreover, a uniform federal law would not necessarily be more stable or predictable than the current system. As members of Congress change, so do the wishes of their constituents. A standard that pleases today's Congress might not appeal to the next. Any federal bill will reflect merely the preferences of a particular Congress, whose members are subject to the influences of lobbyists and campaign contributors, as well as changing constituents. Certain interest groups might unduly influence the contents of the federal uniform law. History shows that these groups will advocate vigorously for their particular cause whenever new laws are being debated.

Federal product liability bills tend to restrict remedies for plaintiffs.

For decades, the powerful business lobby in Washington has said that tort reforms are desperately needed. On closer inspection, though, the phrase "tort reform" usually means changes that favor one side, namely businesses and manufacturers. The provisions in various national reform bills and individual legislation tend to reduce individual rights by moving away from strict liability, limiting damage awards (especially punitive damages), and lowering the statute of limitations so that people have less time to bring lawsuits.

Some provisions allow manufacturers to avoid liability if their products meet standards set by federal regulatory agencies, such as the Food and Drug Administration (FDA), the National Highway Traffic Safety Administration (NHTSA), and others. Provisions like these make it harder for injured parties to hold wrongdoers responsible. Injustices can occur when companies are able to hide behind a federal preemption.

Since Congress passed the Medical Device Amendment of 1976, which gives certain exemptions from product liability, injured people have had trouble collecting damages when they are injured or killed by a medical device approved by the FDA. In two 1993 cases, courts allowed this defense when women tried to sue a company that made collagen used in medical practice. The plaintiffs had developed autoimmune diseases, which they attributed to the collagen. The courts, however, ruled that the Medical Device Amendment protected the collagen makers from lawsuits, since the FDA had approved their product.[10]

Speaking to Congress about these cases, attorney Bruce A. Finzen raised important concerns about this kind of federal law:

> The courts . . . reached these decisions in spite of evidence of fraud upon the FDA by the manufacturers of the device. The courts also ignored the FDA's own regulation interpreting the Medical Device Amendment as not preempting state tort laws. Finally, the courts reached their results with full knowledge that the Medical Device Amendment provides no remedy for monetary compensation to individuals injured by medical devices.[11]

QUOTABLE

President Gerald Ford

[The Medical Device Amendment of 1976] is also important as a symbol for the kind of regulation that I feel is most appropriate to government. It does not represent another expansion of government into affairs we might better manage ourselves. Instead, this is an example of government doing for the individual citizen what he or she cannot do unaided.

Source: President Gerald Ford, "Statement on Signing the Medical Device Amendments of 1976," May 28, 1976, http://www.presidency.ucsb.edu/ws/index.php?pid=6069.

Courts and state lawmakers protect consumers by addressing problems more efficiently than the federal government.

Over the course of more than 30 years, Congress has spent many hours considering comprehensive product liability bills but has failed to pass any of them. Federal regulatory agencies often move slowly too, but sometimes they move too quickly to approve a product that later is found to be harmful.

While performing their judicial duties, courts provide an important public service by addressing matters the federal government might address too slowly, too hastily, or not at all. When lawmakers in Washington do not act to improve product safety through the political process, attorneys say they are justified in using the court system to protect consumers. Attorneys who sued the tobacco companies in mass class-action suits say that Congress failed to do enough to regulate this industry. Those who decided to sue gun manufacturers have likewise pointed to federal inaction.

The U.S. Supreme Court has sanctioned a state's right to promote safety within its borders. In 1985, the Court wrote, "Throughout our history the several States have exercised their police powers to protect the health and safety of their citizens. Because these are 'primarily, and historically ... matter[s] of local concern.'"[12] That same year, the Court wrote, "States traditionally have had great latitude under their police powers to legislate as to the protection of the lives, limbs, health, comfort, and quiet of all persons."[13]

Allowing such cases to be heard in local courts with judges and juries is a vital part of the system. Working along with the regulatory processes, courts help to keep people safer. Lawsuits immediately put companies on notice that their product has caused an injury. Knowing that they might be sued, companies are more careful in designing and making products. If they are sued, they can recall the product or issue safety warnings to people who bought it.

Letting different states develop their own policies allows experimentation with new and innovative solutions. Diverse approaches let people see how different solutions work before the solutions are implemented in too many places at once. Approaches that prove effective can be tried elsewhere, while policies that work well in only one part of the country need not be widely used.

A non-uniform approach may involve certain trade-offs, but it works better in the long run. Courts are better able to adjust to changes in state law than to sweeping federal mandates. Once federal laws are in place, they are more difficult to change than regional case laws. Ill-founded laws may remain in place too long. A new law that is flawed can cause a lot of damage throughout the nation before it is changed.

Supporters of federal action say federal agencies can adequately protect consumers. Though they may try their best, federal agencies often lack the resources to fully investigate every potential product or track every developing problem and then conduct the necessary hearings to deal with it. The FDA, for example, must carry out comprehensive pre- and post-market inspections for products, yet often the agency is under pressure to approve these products quickly. Critics note situations in which the FDA did not uncover potential dangers. Unsafe pharmaceuticals and medical devices have received approval and caused harm before they were removed. The FDA approved DES (diethylstilbestrol) for use in 1941, for example. It was approved

QUOTABLE

Justice Louis Brandeis

It is one of the happy incidents of the federal system that a single courageous state may, if its citizens choose, serve as a laboratory; and try novel social and economic experiments without risk to the rest of the country.

Source: *New State Ice Co. v. Liebmann*, 285 U.S. 262, 311 (1932).

for use during pregnancy to prevent miscarriages, but later this pharmaceutical was linked to health problems in the children of women who took it, including vaginal cancer and abnormalities in reproductive organs. Studies conducted during the 1960s then showed that DES was not even effective in preventing miscarriages. Federal agencies charged with food safety responsibilities only are able to inspect less than 2 percent of the imported food products that are sold in the United States.[14] Through the years, numerous tainted food products have been consumed before officials knew something was wrong.

Monitoring business practices and the safety of products all over the country is a huge job. The courts and state governments must play a continuing role in this process, unimpeded by rigid federal laws. Consumers, too, have a role, as they bring unsafe products to the attention of the courts.

Summary

It would be unwise to replace two centuries of common law and state statutes with uniform national product liability laws, especially since critics cannot prove that the current system does not work. Congress had recognized the problems of a uniform approach as it considered and then failed to pass several comprehensive product liability laws in recent decades. Citizens are likely to feel disenfranchised if sweeping federal laws are enacted that would prevent their elected officials from addressing local concerns.

Such a universal law also would raise constitutional issues. Congress is not authorized to supervise the court system or to control judicial inquiry. The Founding Fathers understood the need for diverse approaches and the vibrant development of the law throughout the nation. In its decisions, the U.S. Supreme Court also has avoided making rigid rules that all courts must use for product liability cases. Instead, the Court has recognized state and judicial sovereignty because democracy must continue to thrive at the local level.

Strict Liability Standards Cause Economic Problems

Product laws have evolved to the extent that manufacturers increasingly face liability regardless of fault or negligence. Since the 1960s, most courts have applied strict liability. Using a negligence standard, courts supported the idea that individuals are responsible for harms caused by their product only if they could have reasonably prevented that harm. With strict liability, they can be held liable even if they could not have reasonably foreseen that harm.

Strict liability leads to high costs for litigation and insurance, and these higher costs make U.S. products more expensive. As a result, domestic businesses are less competitive in the global markets and companies have less money available for growth, research, and development. Damage awards from these lawsuits redistribute wealth in ways that burden both businesses and citizens. Strict liability departs too far from the standards of negligence and due care on the part of defendants, and it does not pay enough attention to misbehavior by plaintiffs. Because anyone can be sued, defendants can include any party in the chain of distribution of a product, any of which faces heavy burdens in court. Additionally, plaintiffs have been able to collect damages even when they were negligent themselves or when they misused a product. For example, damages have been collected from makers of automobile parts for crashes that occurred while plaintiffs were driving over the speed limit, under the influence of alcohol, or without seatbelts.[1]

Strict liability gives the plaintiff unfair advantages.

Manufacturers often cannot predict what a court will regard as a "defect," which makes it difficult to prevent injuries or to provide warnings that a court will consider adequate. As Justice Benjamin Cardozo said in 1916, "There must be knowledge of a danger, not merely possible, but probable. It is possible to use almost anything in a way that will make it dangerous if defective. That is not enough to charge the manufacturer with a duty independent of his contract."[2]

When the focus is on finding someone to pay for an individual's injuries, courts are less inclined to fairly draw reasonable conclusions about whether a manufacturer performed its proper duties. This can be seen in cases where courts give too broad a reading to the word *defective*. A manufacturer can follow or even exceed industry standards or mandatory federal standards yet still be held liable. Courts have held companies liable not because their product was made in a negligent way but because the design did not meet a more ideal standard. This process often involves plenty of hindsight. The risks that emerge *after* an accident tend to seem more obvious than they had been when the product was launched. The product might have been state-of-the-art at that time. Perhaps no feasible design alternative was then available, and the manufacturer lacked the power or knowledge to prevent the so-called defect.

Juries also can consider each feature of a product in isolation. They may not understand how changing one aspect would require other changes that could make the product less effective or even less safe. A manufacturer also might be expected to make two or more changes that are incompatible with one another or that go against federal standards. In some cases, companies are told to change aspects of a product's design in ways that conflict with a court's ruling in another case. For example, car manufacturers have placed gas tanks in different places, including the front of, rear of, and underneath the car. Depending on where a car is hit during an accident, any of these locations might be "safe" versus "unsafe." Manufacturers can find themselves in a lose-lose situation, no matter which design they chose.

The high costs of strict liability cause negative economic consequences for businesses and consumers.

Strict liability has increased the costs of doing business for both small and large companies. Unusually high damage awards have become commonplace. From 1996 to 2003, the average size of jury verdicts in accident cases doubled to more than $1.2 million.[3] From 1992 to 2005, the median damage award in state courts in the nation's 75 most populous counties increased from $154,000 to $749,000.[4] In 2004, the median jury award in product liability cases was $1.8 million.[5]

Higher damage awards mean higher insurance premiums. The American Tort Reform Association (ATRA) notes that product liability insurance premiums have risen at twice the rate of inflation in recent years.[6] Even companies that have never faced a product liability claim are paying higher premiums and also are paying more for less coverage. The president of a company that makes interior furnishings said, "While we do not suffer the liability exposure of, say, a lawnmower manufacturer, we are still forced to carry many millions of dollars in liability insurance. The cost of this insurance significantly impacts our operating cost and increases virtually monthly due to the increased costs of other manufacturers in the 'pool.'"[7]

Pacific Research Institute (PRI), a free-market think tank based in California, said that the United States has been spending 2.2 percent of its gross domestic product (GDP) annually on direct tort costs, much higher than Germany (1.1 percent), Japan (0.8 percent), and the United Kingdom (0.7 percent).[8] One source says liability costs in the United States are 15 times greater than in Japan and 20 times greater than in Europe.[9] This means that domestic components and finished products cost more than their foreign counterparts.

When American businesses struggle to compete in the global economy, jobs are lost. They are also lost when companies must close because they cannot afford insurance. Companies that make beneficial products have been forced out of business, canceled new products, or chosen not to acquire other companies because their insurance bills were too high. For example, a company in Virginia made hand and foot driving controls for disabled drivers. The Veteran's Administration had endorsed the product. Although this company was never sued successfully, it still had to close after its liability insurance premiums rose during the mid-1980s. Some companies, especially small businesses, even have declared bankruptcy after losing a product liability case.

The high costs of liability insurance and lawsuits have led many U.S. firms to limit their product lines and raise prices. As a result, say analysts, consumers have a more limited choice of domestic products at higher prices, and American products are less competitive abroad.[10] According to the Pacific Research Institute, American businesses suffer an estimated $367 billion in lost product sales because the costs of litigation curtail research and development.[11] In addition to economic costs, executives spend large chunks of time each year on liability problems.

The costs—from insurance, attorney and lawsuit fees, and the need to develop warnings designed to limit liability—are passed on to consumers. According to a publication from the National Small Business Association (NSBA), in 2001, the average family of four in the United States was paying a "litigation tax" of almost $2,900 for products and services.[12] In a report issued in 2007, the Pacific Research Institute calculated this amount at $7,848.[13]

As one example, the cost of the "tort tax" in the ladder manufacturing industry was estimated at 20 percent of the cost of each household stepladder.[14] David Golden, director of commercial lines for the Property Casualty Insurers Association of America, notes: "Every time you purchase food, clothing, cars, toys, or anything else, a portion of what you pay goes to cover the cost of lawsuits."[15]

Some people think that passing liability costs on to a large number of consumers is good public policy. This ignores the fact that a price increase, even a small one, may lead consumers to stop purchasing the product or to buy a cheaper product from abroad, where manufacturers have lower product liability costs.

All American consumers are, in effect, paying something like a tax that is then used to pay a relatively small number of plaintiffs and their lawyers. These payouts are made even though most people already have health insurance to cover the costs for their medical treatment if they are injured. Most courts do not consider these other payments, such as health insurance, when they make compensatory damage awards to winning plaintiffs. Critics say that this quasi-tax is illegal, since it comes from court decisions, not legislation.

Supporters of strict liability claim this approach saves time and money by making it easier for courts to decide cases. The standard is lower than it would be in a negligence case, so the court only needs to determine that the product in question caused the plaintiff's injury. This might shorten an individual trial, but strict liability means that many more lawsuits are brought. That increases court costs in the long run.

Threats and actual lawsuits discourage companies from expanding, innovating, and introducing new products.

In a Senate hearing on a bill to reform product liability laws, the owner of an Illinois-based sports equipment company said:

> A couple of years ago, we designed a new baseball product. We "mocked up" the product and ran the prototype through all the safety tests. It produced great results. We were very excited about the innovation. But when we looked into full scale production, we could not get anyone to supply us with the needed materials.[16]

These suppliers feared product liability lawsuits in which they might be named as defendants along with the company that was making the sports equipment. As of 1994, only two companies in the United States still were making football helmets, as compared to 18 such companies in 1970.[17]

Many other companies face similar dilemmas in developing promising new products. In a letter to the National Association of Manufacturers, a New Jersey company wrote that the high cost of product liability and insurance "forces a company like ours to withdraw products and abandon research and development for new ones. We are forced to watch our international competitors developing products we ourselves had hoped to manufacture and sell."[18] Even when companies successfully defend a product lawsuit, they may be unable to obtain insurance because of the high costs of defending these suits, including those that are dismissed or settled out of court.

Liability issues also caused serious problems for the nation's private aircraft industry. U.S. companies produced 17,811 private planes in 1978, but that number declined by more than 90 percent between 1979 and 1990, when the cost of liability added an average of $100,000 to the cost of each plane. Some companies, such as Cessna, stopped producing planes. According to product liability expert W. Kip Viscusi, "Aircraft companies are sued in 90 percent of all crashes involving fatalities or serious injury, even though pilot error is responsible for 85 percent of all accidents."[19] As a result, the price of new planes goes up, and older planes remain in use. This effect is ironic in terms of safety, as Viscusi notes, because older planes are more likely to fail than newer models. The government stepped in with the General Aviation Revitalization Act of 1994. That year, only 928 new U.S.-made general aviation planes were shipped. The numbers have risen (to 2,137 in 2003), but they remain much lower than they were before 1980.[20]

Product liability also has strongly impacted the pharmaceutical industry. Henry Grabowski notes: "The evidence is mounting that this situation is growing worse in the United States. Our experience appears to be in sharp contrast to that of most other developed countries."[21] Grabowski cites evidence that these companies are less willing to pursue research and development for new products because of liability concerns in important therapeutic categories.[22]

Drug manufacturers have discontinued materials people found beneficial because of excessive liability costs. Searle Laboratories discontinued an intrauterine birth control device called the Copper-7 (Cu-7). This device went through extensive testing with more than 16,000 women before the FDA approved it, but Searle then faced lawsuits from women who alleged the device had caused infections and other problems, including infertility. [23] Searle spent $1.5 million defending four lawsuits in 1985. Though it won all four cases, the company decided the product was too vulnerable to lawsuits, so it was unprofitable to sell it. The editors of *Developing New Contraceptives* write, "From the evidence available to the committee, we conclude that recent products liability litigation and the impact of that litigation on the cost and availability of liability insurance have contributed significantly to the climate of disincentives for the development of contraceptive products."[24] As a result, say the authors, the United States fell about a decade behind Europe in this area of medicine.

Strict liability puts too little responsibility on the consumer.

Plaintiffs should be accountable when their own behavior causes a product injury. All too often, courts ignore or excuse various kinds of contributory negligence on the part of the plaintiff. These include reckless use, lack of product maintenance, or the disregard of operating instructions and posted and/or printed warnings that come with a product. Misuse of a product should be considered as a viable defense, yet people have won cases after they changed products in ways that made them less safe.

Critics note that manufacturers have paid large damages in cases in which consumers themselves were not careful or failed to supervise their children. These include cases in which children accidentally started fires after they picked up disposable lighters or babies who drowned after parents left them alone in a baby tub in a larger bathtub of water.

Consumers often have very unreasonable expectations. In *The Case Against Lawyers*, Catherine Crier writes:

QUOTABLE

We were faced with a personal injury law suit filed by a user who did not follow instructions or use common sense when using the product. To minimize attorneys' fees, we settled the suit out of court. The injury sustained by the plaintiff was a few stitches in his arm.

—From a letter written by a Colorado company, included in a statement by the National Association of Manufacturers before Congress, February 2, 1993

Source: http://www.archive.org/stream/s687productliabi00unit/
s687productliabi00unit_djvu.txt.

[Kmart recalled 24,000 teakettles] because of fourteen reports of "boiling water improperly expelled from the spout" that could present a hazard. Three cases of minor burns were included in those incidents. The last time I poured boiling water from an open pan, it did the same thing. My teakettle produces hot steam that will burn me if I get in the way during pouring. Should I turn these items in?[25]

In the Product Liability Reform Act of 1997, Congress recognized the need for reasonable behavior by consumers. The bill (which did not become law) suggested several defenses to product liability, based on the plaintiff's wrongful actions. They included:

The defendant has a complete defense if the plaintiff was under the influence of intoxicating alcohol or illegal drugs and as a result of this influence was more than 50 percent responsible for the plaintiff's injuries. . . .

A defendant's liability is reduced to the extent a claimant's harm is due to the misuse or alteration of a product.[26]

People also should not be allowed to sue companies for injuries that occur with products that are too old or worn-out to work properly. These products have passed their normal lifespan. At some point, liability should cease.

Recently, enterprising attorneys decided to sue on behalf of groups of people who are obese. They targeted fast-food companies, claiming that these companies were responsible for their clients' weight problems and the health problems that often accompany obesity. Individuals also have sued fast-food restaurants, claiming they had a duty to warn their patrons that eating this kind of food several times a week could cause them to become overweight. Such litigation raises serious questions about personal responsibility.

Strict liability does not ensure safer products or fewer injuries.

Has strict liability brought safer products and lower accident rates? When George Priest studied statistics gathered during the 1980s, when the number of product liability suits rose sharply, he found that injury and death rates did not decline any faster than in the 1970s, when fewer lawsuits occurred. Such events already were declining, and they continued to do so at about the same rate.[27]

Other studies have looked at auto safety. John D. Graham and his colleagues conducted case studies of motor vehicle safety to see how liability affected designs that were meant to produce safer vehicles and to prevent injuries. Their analysis showed that factors other than product liability lawsuits have improved auto safety. Graham writes:

> The regression analysis suggests that the main factors caus-
> ing improved passenger safety since [World War II] have
> been consumer demand (stimulated by rising incomes),
> construction of the highly safe interstate highway system
> (where the amount of travel has grown enormously),
> and vehicle regulation (in the form of the NHTSA safety
> standards).... Trends in product liability law appear
> to have had an insignificant influence on passenger car
> death rates compared with other major forces.[28]

Graham also notes, "The case studies provide little evidence that expanded product liability risk was necessary to achieve the safety improvements that have been made.... The combined effects of consumer demand, regulation, and professional responsibility would have been sufficient to achieve improved safety."[29] Finally, Graham contended that manufacturers wanted to make products that gave them a good reputation in the marketplace: "Manufacturers strive to avoid the adverse reputational consequences that highly publicized liability actions can produce."[30]

Product liability expert W. Kip Viscusi notes that from 1985 to 1989, the number of product liability suits in the federal courts increased, as did the amounts of the awards. Yet accident rates declined. Data that the National Safety Council collected from 1977 to 1987 showed a 20 percent decline in total accident rates, an 11 percent decline in motor vehicle accident rates, a 25 percent decline in work accident rates, and a 26 percent decline in home accident rates. During those same years, litigation rates rose sharply.[31] From 1980 to 2001, general liability costs in the United States increased from $6.4 billion to $22 billion, yet the overall accidental death rate per 100,000 people decreased from 46.2 to 35.3.[32]

Advances in technology, market forces, and state and federal regulations affect product safety. Common sense tells us that companies *want* to produce safe and effective products in order to please consumers and to stay in business. Numerous state and federal agencies set standards and oversee certain industries and products. Certain products, such as pharmaceuticals, must be approved before they can be marketed. Other products are inspected to make sure they are safe, and the government will ask for a recall if problems occur. The federal government continues to find ways to improve product safety.

Strict liability actually can work against safety. In some places, if employers have removed safety devices that the manufacturer put on the machine, injured employees can still sue the manufacturer under strict liability. This goes against the idea of maintaining safe products. If employers were held liable instead, this could make the workplace safer. People also might take more care in reading instructions if they know other people will not be liable for carelessness on their part.

Another question arises: Should everyone pay higher prices because some people are not careful? The cost of producing totally safe products could result in products that are too expensive for most consumers. It also can mean fewer products in the marketplace. In his article "The Mirage of Product Safety," John Hasnas writes:

Because safety is an inherently subjective concept, there is no general standard that can guarantee each consumer his or her desired level of safety at a price he or she would be willing to pay. Only a market can do

THE LETTER OF THE LAW

Consumer Product Safety Improvement Act of 2008

On August 14, 2008, President George W. Bush signed into law the Consumer Product Safety Improvement Act of 2008. The CPSIA grants the Consumer Product Safety Commission (CPSC) new resources and authority, establishes mandatory testing on all children's products, bans lead in children's toys, and aims to inform the public more quickly when potential problems come to light:

Title I - Children's Product Safety
Section 101 -

Treats as a banned hazardous substance under the Federal Hazardous Substances Act (FHSA) any children's product (a consumer product designed or intended primarily for children 12 years of age or younger) containing more than specified amounts of lead....

Section 102 -

Amends the Consumer Product Safety Act (CPSA) to revise requirements regarding manufacturer certification of products subject to a safety rule as being compliant with safety standards with provisions requiring a manufacturer of a product that is subject to a safety rule to certify that, based on a test of each product or on a reasonable testing program, the product complies with all rules, bans, standards, or regulations applicable to the product under the CPSA or any other CPSC-enforced Act....

Section 103 -

Requires the manufacturer of a children's product to label the product and its packaging, to the extent practicable, to identify the product's location and date of production and cohort information....

Section 108 -

Makes it unlawful to manufacture, sell, distribute, or import a children's toy or child care article containing specified concentrations of specified phthalates....

Source: http://www.govtrack.us/congress/bill.xpd?bill=h110-4040&tab=summary.

this. This explains why the duty that manufacturers have—the duty not to produce deceptively dangerous products—derives directly from the basic requirement for a well-functioning market, which is the duty of honest dealing.[33]

The ambiguous "duty to warn" leads to excessive warnings, higher costs, and unfair rulings.

The duty to warn has expanded in unpredictable ways. False or misleading labeling is obviously wrong, and the courts have long held people accountable for this kind of misdeed. But labeling expectations should be reasonable. In the McMahon case mentioned in the Introduction, the plaintiffs said that although they knew hot coffee could cause burns if spilled, they should have been warned that the burns would be severe. The Indiana court said this kind of information could not likely be posted on a coffee maker.[34]

To protect themselves, many companies incur extra costs by creating extensive instructions and warning labels. Labels now include information that covers even remote possibilities. For example, buyers of toilet brushes have been warned not to use the product for personal hygiene, while instructions for baby strollers tell people to remove the child before folding the stroller. Debra Rae Anderson writes:

> Ironically, 90 percent of product liability cases aren't based on a defective product, but rather are brought to court on the basis that the manufacturer didn't warn against all possible dangers. As a result, warning labels cover every product on the market. The warning label on a step ladder is almost a foot long and the warning labels on children's toys have reached a point of ridiculousness. Kids' plastic play fire hats say "not to be used as a protective helmet," and Batman costumes warn that "cape does not enable user to fly." How far will we force manufacturers to go in order to protect themselves against lawsuits?[35]

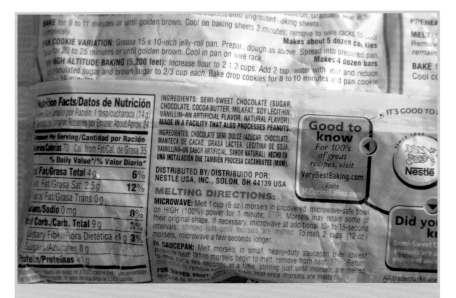

Although warning labels have been a great source of controversy in product liability cases, Penny Ackerman was grateful for the warning label on this bag of chocolate chips, which explained they were made in a facility that also processes peanuts. Her young son Gregory is extremely allergic to peanuts.

In some cases, people have been sued for not posting information that seems like common knowledge. Manufacturers of alcohol have been sued for failing to post warnings about the dangers of alcoholism. Tire makers have been sued for not giving adequate warnings about the risks of underinflated tires. An Indiana woman won a jury verdict for $485,000 when she was injured after her chaise lounge collapsed. She had not opened the chair fully, and the jury concluded that the company had a duty to explain in the instructions that this chair might collapse under those conditions.[36] In that case, the court looked at whether the danger was "open and obvious" and concluded that under a strict liability standard, "if people generally believe that there is a danger associated with the use of a product, but that there is a safe way to use it, any danger there may be in using the product in the way generally believed to be safe is not open and obvious."[37]

Excessive warnings could distract consumers from paying close attention to those warnings that provide important new information against less obvious dangers. A federal court noted this problem in 1993:

> Extended warnings present several difficulties, first among them that, the more text must be squeezed onto the product, the smaller the type, and the less likely is the consumer to read or remember any of it. Only pithy and bold warnings can be effective. Long passages in capital letters are next to illegible, and long passages in lower case letters are treated as boilerplate. Plaintiff wants a warning in such detail that a magnifying glass would be necessary to read it.[38]

A strict liability standard lets people claim they did not know about things most people know. To prevent such situations, reformers suggest using a negligence or fraud standard in regard to warnings, and some states have passed laws to that effect. Others say that a uniform national labeling standard is the answer.

QUOTABLE

Catherine Crier, Journalist and Attorney

The law must be reasonable. It is not. Labels now warn us against the most absurd events. A thirteen-inch wheel on a wheelbarrow warns "not intended for highway use" while an electric router for carpenters says "This product not intended for use as a dental drill."

Source: Catherine Crier, *The Case Against Lawyers: How the Lawyers, Politicians, and Bureaucrats Have Turned the Law Into an Instrument of Tyranny and What We as Citizens Have to Do About It.* New York: Random House, 2003, p. 3.

Summary

Strict liability has become much too broad, imposing far too many duties on businesses and too little responsibility on plaintiffs. The current system offers great potential for abuse, fraud, and exaggeration. Plaintiffs can collect even if they acted irresponsibly. Strict liability encourages more lawsuits, many of them unwarranted. Defendants pay whether they were negligent or not. Defending a case costs time and money, even if the case is dismissed.

A better approach would focus on true defects in a product that cause harm when the product is in its original condition and has been used in a normal and reasonable manner for a time that does not exceed its normal life. Courts would apply standards of reasonably foreseeable behavior and due care to product warnings and instructions.

Support for strict liability has waned in recent decades. In *Product Liability*, author Jane Stapleton writes, "Earlier academic enthusiasm for, and confidence in, stricter tort liability for products has given way in many cases to a pessimism about both the theory and practice of the rule." After analyzing academic writings on this subject, Stapleton says that "virtually all eminent scholars now agree that liability for design and warning cases is and should be fault-based."[39]

Strict Liability Standards Protect People

During the second half of the twentieth century, a standard of strict liability filled gaps in product liability law that once prevented injured people from being compensated. This standard has required manufacturers to do more to keep consumers safe. Critics want a higher standard of proof for injured plaintiffs and think manufacturers should be able to avoid liability by putting more responsibilities on the injured party. Those who would turn back the clock toward a more restricted view of product liability want to give advantages to businesses at the expense of consumers.

By the 1940s, American courts were moving toward a standard of strict liability. This approach helps protect victims' rights, makes it easier for injured parties to have their day in court and to recover damages, and keeps people safe by providing strong incentives for companies to make products that do not cause harm and to provide effective warning labels.

Strict liability recognizes that manufacturing businesses have far more power than consumers. Businesses are able to make and sell their products to mass markets, advertise through the media with little supervision, and make claims without proving them. People who buy products do not always have the information they need to judge manufacturers' products. For these and other reasons, strict liability is the appropriate standard for legal cases involving products.

Critics exaggerate problems in the strict liability approach.

In 2004, a Tennessee court heard a case in which a halogen torchiere lamp caught fire after a child put a pillow on it. The mother sued the manufacturer, claiming that the lamp was dangerous or defective after it was made or sold. The court disagreed, saying that the lamp was not "unreasonably dangerous," and ruled for the company.[1]

Critics of strict liability would have everyone believe that this case and others like it would naturally be decided in favor of the plaintiffs. They contend that courts give damages to anyone who complains about a product or has even a minor injury. To support the idea of a "crisis" in product liability law, critics talk about frivolous lawsuits and exaggerate the number of cases and the amounts of the awards. The public hears about unusual cases that give a distorted view designed to make plaintiffs look unworthy. All too often, the public does not hear about victims who were clearly entitled to the damages they received. Inundated with half-truths and misrepresentations, we are encouraged to see only problems in the system.

Statistics show that product liability cases are less common than people think. One study published by the Rand Corporation found that only about 10 percent of the people injured by a product file a claim for compensation.[2] From 1992 to 2005, the number of product liability trials in state courts in the nation's 75 most populous counties declined from 657 to 225.[3]

Reform advocates also say the nation is in a "litigation crisis," but the number of tort cases actually has been declining. The National Center for State Courts (NCSC) found that from 1996 to 2000, the number of tort cases fell from 320,976 cases to 260,745 cases in 16 states.[4] When the NCSC looked at activities in 35 states, it saw a decline of 4 percent from 1992 to 2002. (The total population in these states is about 77 percent of the U.S. population as a whole.) Moreover, the number of tort cases filed *per capita* also had declined, going from 230 per 100,000 residents in 1975 to 212 per 100,000 in 2000.[5]

Damage awards are lower than many people think, and they often are reduced after the trial. One study showed that larger awards were reduced, on average, to about 57 percent of the original award. For other cases, on average, the amount was reduced to about 71 percent of the original award.[6] In recent years, damage awards have been fewer as well as lower. The RAND Institute for Civil Justice (ICJ) has found that jury awards are rising in line with the rate of inflation as well as the increased cost of compensating the victims for their medical expenses.[7]

Critics have claimed that the current tort system in the United States costs hundreds of billions of dollars each year. For instance, in 2003, one source estimated the cost was $246 billion.[8] These numbers can be misleading, since this sum also includes payments in tort settlements. Tort settlement payments go from the defendants or their insurance companies to the injured party, not to court costs. Almost half of the 2003 estimated total came from these payments, so these are not costs the public is paying for litigation. Approximately 22 percent went to administrative costs for insurance companies, and that number would not vary if the system changed from strict liability to a weaker form of liability.[9]

Critics try to convince people that strict liability laws hurt the economy by leading to higher insurance costs, more business closings, job losses, a lack of innovation, and problems competing in the global marketplace. A survey by the Risk and Insurance Management Society (RIMS), however, found that many businesses were paying *less than 1 percent* of their total revenues for liability costs.[10] About two-thirds of the companies reported that liability costs made up about 1 percent of the final cost of their products. Another 11 percent said that liability costs accounted for 2 to 3 percent of the final product price.[11]

The U.S. Office of Technology Assessment (OTA) has said that other factors are more crucial to making American businesses more competitive, including a lower cost of capital for business loans and improvements in the education system. Besides, if the U.S. product liability system were so burdensome, why would so many foreign businesses seek to locate here?

Some analysts note that while companies complain about the high costs of strict liability on their businesses, they paint a brighter picture in their financial documents. According to Ralph Nader, these companies include Dow Chemical Co., Corning Inc., Monsanto, and Cessna Aircraft Co. Nader says that on its 10-K form, Monsanto said that product liability laws were not a big economic problem for the company.[12]

QUOTABLE

Ralph Nader

These companies and their trade associations grossly exaggerate product liability costs in their presentations to Congress and to the public in order to advance their agenda of rolling back liability for and records disclosure of their dangerous products. Yet their official financial statements filed with the SEC and distributed to investors disclaim any adverse material effects of product liability on the bottom line.

Source: "Ralph Nader on Tort Reform," *Legal Times*, 1995, http://www.lectlaw.com/files/civ03.htm.

Although critics say the current system requires companies to spend large sums on liability insurance, insurance premiums appear, on average, to be a small part of a business's overall budget. The National Insurance Consumer Organization (NICO) reported that in 1991 product liability insurance premiums that were paid as a percent of product retail sales amounted to 14 percent.[13] NICO concluded, "For the major corporations surveyed, the pressures of product liability have hardly affected larger economic issues, such as revenues, market share or employee retention."[14] Higher insurance rates since the late 1990s can be attributed to other causes besides product liability: two economic recessions; declines in the stock market; and low long-term interest rates, which reduce investment income for many companies. Likewise, there is no proof that strict liability laws stifle innovation. The data people use to support this claim may be based on faulty evidence, theories, or opinions expressed by people who want to change liability laws.

Critics overlook the fact that using a negligence standard instead of strict liability increases administrative costs. Courts must work harder to determine negligence, since that kind of finding requires two steps: determining the optimal level of care the defendant should have taken, and then determining whether or not the defendant met that level of care. Under strict liability, a court need only conclude that the defendant's product caused the plaintiff's injuries. This can make a court's job easier, especially in complex cases in which it is difficult to determine what precautions a manufacturer should have taken. Using strict liability saves court costs by making the process faster and more efficient.

Strict liability promotes safety by holding companies accountable.

Common sense tells us that holding manufacturers responsible for their products will encourage them to make them safer. If defendants can say they were not negligent or at fault, they have less incentive to spend time and money on safety. They also may use a risk/benefit approach and decide that their liability is low enough that they will not add certain safety features for cost reasons. Experts and research studies agree with these conclusions. In their testimony before the Senate, MIT professors Nicholas Ashford and Robert Stone stated that tort liability promotes safety, encourages innovations that are safer, and discourages unsafe innovations.[15]

The Conference Board, Inc.—a business-information service that consults with senior executives about management practices and economic and public policy—examined how product liability influences corporate decisions. After surveying 232 risk managers at large U.S. corporations, this group concluded:

> Where product liability has had a notable impact—where it has most significantly affected management decision making—has been in the quality of the products themselves. Managers say products have become safer, manufacturing procedures have been improved, and labels and use instructions have become more explicit.[16]

W. Kip Viscusi and Michael J. Moore concluded that tort liability had "safety incentive effects." They write, "Higher levels of liability costs usually increase product-related research and development."[17]

Businesses and insurers complain that the system is too unpredictable, since they cannot be sure how much a court will award in damages to the plaintiff. According to consumer advocate Ralph Nader, this is one of the greatest benefits of strict liability because "this unpredictability is the very essence of deterrence—a function of the civil justice system which is just as important as compensation and which, like the system's other social benefits, cannot be precisely quantified in dollars and cents."[18]

Consumers certainly can have more confidence in products that come from a nation with high safety standards. Critics who say strict liability hurts the economy and makes it harder for American businesses to compete globally ignore this important benefit. In 1990, Professor Mark Hager of American University told Congress:

> [American] products, because of their superior repu-
> tation for safety, due in part to the effects of product
> liability over the last 20 years, have a superior reputa-
> tion in the international marketplace. . . . [W]e cannot
> compete at this time with the low labor costs of newly
> industrializing countries, but we can compete very
> effectively . . . in safety, and it would be a grave risk
> to our international competitiveness to toy with the
> tort system that helps bring about that competitive
> advantage.[19]

Strict liability is fairer for consumers—and good public policy.

Strict liability places responsibility on those best situated to guard against defects and assume the risk: manufacturers who have the capacity to research, test, and improve their products in development. They are able to provide safety features during the manufacturing process and to develop sound warnings and instructions.

A strict liability system fits the nation's ideals of equal justice under the law. Using strict liability standards levels the playing field for consumers. Wealthy corporations exert influence through powerful lobbies, campaign contributions, and allies in high places. An individual cannot as easily influence what government will do. Through the legal system, however, ordinary Americans can require even a powerful corporation to account for its actions. Without a strict liability standard, many injured parties might be unable to collect damages.

Critics must remember that when businesses pay product liability damages, they are not being punished for misdeeds.

Rather, as George G. Brenkert notes, "This compensation is a way to restore competitive balance in the marketplace. . . . The manufacturer's product caused the injury and the manufacturer still profited unfairly from the sale of the defective product."[20]

This aligns with good public policy. Though manufacturers may not have caused the injury on purpose or through negligence, who is better able to bear the cost—the manufacturer or the injured person? The potential for risk was set in motion by the manufacturer's decision to make and sell the product. In the absence of strict liability, injured persons can be stuck with these costs as if they merely resulted from bad luck, not from the product.

Justice Roger J. Traynor noted these benefits in the case of *Escola v. Coca-Cola Bottling Co.*: "The cost of an injury and the loss of time or health may be an overwhelming misfortune to the person injured, and a needless one, for the risk of injury can be insured by the manufacturer and distributed among the public as a cost of doing business."[21] Justice Traynor saw that companies often spread the risk to the general population in the form of slightly higher prices, which costs only a small amount for each consumer. David G. Owen and Jerry Phillips write, "Because modern science and technology benefit society as a whole, all consumers can fairly be asked to pay slightly higher prices as premiums for insurance against the risk of often random harm when science and technology go awry."[22] In effect, this indirectly gives all consumers "mandatory accident insurance for harm from product defects."[23]

Applying strict liability to the labeling of products is likewise beneficial and does not overburden companies. Courts are able to sort out reasonable versus unreasonable conduct when it comes to warning labels and instructions. For example, a man who suffered liver damage when he took Tylenol won a judgment against the company that makes this medication because the company failed to warn about the dangers of combining Tylenol with alcohol use. In the 2009 case of *Wyeth v. Levine*, the U.S. Supreme Court stated that companies can be held liable even when their labels comply with FDA regulations.

Summary

Strict liability enables people to assert their rights and brings the public's attention to the hazards related to product use. This system compensates injured parties and seeks to prevent others from being harmed. Critics complain about excessive costs, but the focus should be on providing justice. Instead of limiting the ability to sue, manufacturers should make safe products so that people are not injured in the first place. Courts have a key role here, along with administrative agencies.

Returning to older standards of liability is unwise and unnecessary. Courts still can hear evidence on both sides of these cases and draw reasonable lines in terms of what constitutes a safe versus a dangerous product. Any changes in these laws should be based on careful analysis, not on isolated incidents or misleading statistics. State and federal laws should not make it more difficult for injured people to sue and receive compensation.

Strict liability is not the same thing as absolute liability. When people are found liable, strict liability does not find them morally guilty; it merely says that their product caused the injury. As Justice Traynor wrote in 1963 in *Greenman v. Yuba Power Products, Inc.*, "The purpose of such liability is to insure that the costs of injuries resulting from defective products are borne by the manufacturers that put such products on the market rather than by the injured persons who are powerless to protect themselves."[24]

Courts Should Have Less Discretion in Awarding Damages

In 1996, the U.S. Supreme Court ruled on a case that shows how punitive damages awards can run wild. In Alabama, a man sued a car company after he discovered that the paint on his new BMW had been touched up. A jury awarded this plaintiff $4 million in punitive damages. On appeal, the Alabama Supreme Court cut that award to $2 million. BMW appealed the decision to the U.S. Supreme Court, which overturned the $2 million award and called it "excessive."[1] In reaching its decision, the Court noted that the loss of value to the $40,000 car was about $4,000.[2]

This was the first time the nation's highest court had ruled on the matter of excessive punitive damages. Writing for the majority, Justice John Paul Stevens said, "Elementary notions of fairness enshrined in our constitutional jurisprudence dictate that a person receive fair notice not only of the conduct that will subject him to punishment but also of the severity of the penalty that a State may impose."[3] Justice Stevens said the Court would continue to avoid offering any "simple mathematical formula" for determining such damages but noted that "when the ratio is a breathtaking 500 to 1, however, the award must surely raise a suspicious judicial eyebrow."[4]

Critics say that non-economic damages, especially punitive damages, are too unpredictable and often unfair. They say it is much harder to calculate a fair amount for damages that are intended to punish the defendant and to deter such behavior in the future than it is to determine objective losses, such as the cost of medical care, lost wages, or property damage. Punitive awards can vary greatly, even in cases with similar circumstances. For example, in the McDonald's coffee case discussed earlier, the jury based its punitive award of $2.7 million on the amount the company made every two days on coffee sales. Using this formula, a small family-owned store might be assessed less than $100 in punitive damages if a plaintiff won his or her case after suffering similar burns from coffee purchased there.

The idea of imposing punitive damages is not new. Beginning in 1763, English common law recognized that punitive damages were permitted in cases of intentional torts (involving conscious harm)—assault and battery, malicious prosecution, and false imprisonment. In the United States, from the late 1700s through most of the 1900s, only a small number of torts involved punitive damages, and the monetary awards were small. According to the American Tort Reform Association, before 1976 there were just three reported cases in which appeals courts upheld punitive damages awards in product liability lawsuits.[5] Such damages were awarded in cases in which the courts found that manufacturers had marketed unsafe products fraudulently and/ or sold products with a known hazard and failed to disclose this knowledge to potential consumers.

Starting in the late 1970s, product liability standards became stricter, which led to a significant increase in both the number and size of damage awards. Companies—now having fewer defenses—were held liable in a broader range of cases. They were less able to predict what conduct would be punishable and what the scope of that punishment would be.

As punitive damages reached millions and then billions of dollars, people complained that these awards were out of proportion to both the injury and the manufacturer's deeds. Critics say that manufacturers have been forced to pay punitive damages even when they were not guilty of negligence, fraud, or a reckless disregard for people's safety. The goal of providing compensatory damages is to make the injured person "whole," and punitive awards are intended to punish wrongdoing and promote public safety, but in many cases enormous punitive awards go far beyond these goals, and simply make plaintiffs (and their attorneys) wealthy. Clearly, changes are needed to make this process more fair and reasonable and to protect defendants' rights.

The use of punitive damages can violate the defendants' rights.

Critics say that punitive damages have the impact of a criminal proceeding, yet the defendants have fewer rights than people who are accused of a crime. This raises serious questions about the procedures used to award and quantify punitive damages. Critics invoke the Eighth Amendment to the U.S. Constitution, which is intended to protect Americans against excessive fines, and the Fourteenth Amendment, which guarantees due process of law in regard to the taking of property. Punitive damages also can be viewed as a redistribution of wealth and a sort of taxation without representation, since these costs are passed on to consumers in the form of higher prices. This raises other issues, since the legislature has the role of levying taxes.

It is true that the U.S. Supreme Court rejected the due process argument in *Pacific Mutual Life Insurance Co. v. Haslip* (1991). The majority of justices in that case said that punitive damages did not violate the Due Process Clause in that particular case, but that it left the possibility open. Justice Harry A. Blackmun, who wrote the majority opinion, stated that it was possible in some cases for unbridled jury discretion to violate due process when awarding punitive damages. In the *Gore* case, the Court did note that grossly excessive punitive damages can violate a defendant's due process rights. In *Philip Morris v. Williams*, the Court said that a defendant's due process rights can be violated when punitive damages are awarded because of harm done to people other than the plaintiff. This latter case arose after the estate of a heavy smoker who died of lung cancer sued the cigarette maker and won $821,000 in compensatory damages and $79.5 million in punitive damages. The defendant appealed on the basis that the jury had awarded these high punitive damages in order to punish the company for possible damage done to other smokers who were not part of the lawsuit.

How can courts bring more balance and fairness to these proceedings? The U.S. Supreme Court has said that trial courts should be clear with juries about the purpose of punitive damages and that awards should be confined to the defendant's activities within the state so that punitive damages are not "assessed

THE LETTER OF THE LAW

Excerpts from the United States Constitution

Amendment VIII (Ratified as part of the Bill of Rights in 1791)

Excessive bail shall not be required, nor excessive fines imposed, nor cruel or unusual punishments inflicted.

Amendment XIV (Adopted on July 9, 1868)

Section 1

All persons born or naturalized in the United States and subject to the jurisdiction thereof, are citizens of the United States and of the State wherein they reside. No State shall make or enforce any law which shall abridge the privileges or immunities of citizens of the United States; nor shall any State deprive any person of life, liberty, or property, without due process of law; nor deny to any person within its jurisdiction the equal protection of the laws.

Source: http://www.senate.gov/civics/constitution_item/constitution.htm.

for conduct outside the state that may be legal elsewhere."[6] The Court pointed out that this would entail extraterritorial punishment on a defendant, since state laws vary.

Critics of punitive damages argue that plaintiffs ask for punitive damages as a pretext for getting financial information about a defendant. While the defendant's profits are generally considered in setting the amount of punitive damages, they are irrelevant to the determination of compensatory damages. However, having the jury learn how much money the defendant makes—or that the defendant has insurance—can influence a jury to award money to the plaintiff.

Tort reformers criticize state laws that let plaintiff attorneys ask for punitive damages and gain access to a manufacturer's financial records even if the case for punitive damages is weak or nonexistent. They approve of laws passed in California and Minnesota, where a plaintiff must make a *prima facie* argument to show a defendant's liability for punitive damages before gaining access to the defendant's financial information or arguing about the amount of punitive damages before a jury. In other words, the plaintiff must show that if he or she proves the facts alleged, that a legal case for punitive damages would exist. Courts also can split trial issues so that punitive damages are considered separately from liability. Established laws also can withhold the possibility of punitive damages when a company has complied with federal standards, such as those issued by the U.S. Food and Drug Administration (FDA).

Realizing the potential for abuse, courts and legislators have been studying the procedures for awarding punitive damages. Since the 1990s, the U.S. Supreme Court has issued decisions that give judges and juries more direction. The Court has not set absolute limits for these awards but advises that the "ratio of punitive to compensatory awards be reasonable and not unduly large."[7] Some states also have passed legislation to limit punitive damages and have added procedural safeguards, including standards for determining when such damages can be assessed.

Courts should require a high standard of proof before granting punitive damages.

To promote fairness and predictability, courts must uphold the people's right to know what kind of conduct can lead to punishment. Courts should reserve punitive damages for extreme cases that demand high degrees of punishment and deterrence. This is a key part of recognizing the quasi-criminal nature of punitive awards, which can cause great harm to manufacturers and individuals, both financially and in terms of their reputation and future business.

In *BMW v. Gore*, the U.S. Supreme Court recognized that the standard of proof should be high, since people stand to lose so much, by noting that the defendant's conduct must reach a certain "degree of reprehensibility" to justify punitive damages. The Court declared that, in this case, the defendant's conduct was not "sufficiently egregious to justify a punitive sanction that is tantamount to a severe criminal penalty."[8]

Many states have moved from a standard of proof based on a "preponderance of the evidence" to require "clear and convincing proof." According to the American Tort Reform Association, the latter standard offers a middle ground between the usual standard of proof in a civil case ("preponderance of the evidence") and the standard in criminal cases ("beyond a reasonable doubt").[9] This standard has received support from the U.S. Supreme Court, the American Bar Association, the American College of Trial Lawyers, and the National Conference of Commissioners on Uniform State Laws. As of late 2009, this standard had been adopted in 29 states and in the District of Columbia.

Congress also has grappled with this issue. In drafting the Products Liability Reform Act of 1997, legislators set forth the standards they wanted in every state. Under those standards, courts could award punitive damages only if they found that the defendant "wanted to cause serious harm, knew that serious harm would result, or knew that there was a strong probability that serious harm would result."[10] In addition, a court must find that the defendant's conduct was "malicious, dishonest, despicable, or constituted a conscious, flagrant disregard for the rights of others." The bill further provided that the trier of fact (the jury, or a judge in non-jury trials) must find that a punitive award is needed to: "(1) discourage similar wrongful conduct by the defendant or others in like situations; (2) deprive the defendant of any unjustified pecuniary gain derived from the wrongful conduct; or (3) impose an appropriate punishment on the defendant for the wrongful conduct."[11] Since the act's failure, individual states have tackled these issues. The standard in California, for example, says that defendants are subject to punitive damages only if they have shown "despicable conduct." The courts are then allowed to define the term on a case-by-case basis.

New laws can reduce the incentives for bringing unworthy cases or asking for unwarranted punitive damages. Current laws encourage attorneys to push cases even when no intentional misconduct occurred because the rewards can be so great when punitive damages are added.

Reasonable limits can be set on monetary awards.

The standards for fixing the amounts for punitive damages may be vague, and these damages frequently are higher than the awards for actual damages. In an article for the Cato Institute, author Doug Bandow noted that in 1999, the top 10 jury awards to individuals and families all exceeded $100 million—and two of them were more than $1 billion.[12]

Courts have a duty to prevent unreasonable awards, since they can cause harmful economic repercussions, including bankruptcies, job losses, and losses for pension funds. Moreover, a defendant who pays out large punitive damages to a few early plaintiffs may run out of money and cannot even compensate worthy victims who sue them later.

A 1999 case in Alabama shows that juries may even award amounts that far exceed what a plaintiff's attorney proposed. The attorney in the case asked the jury for punitive damages of $6 million, yet they decided on $580 million. (The actual economic damages suffered by the plaintiffs amounted to about $600.) Critics find it hard to imagine how the jury reached this staggering figure, and the jury members did not have to justify it. Cass R. Sunstein notes, "That [$580 million] equals over one and three-quarters times the total annual amount the state of Alabama spends on police protection and correction, including the funding for its prisons."[13]

People obviously differ in what they consider "excessive," but setting standards can help juries and judges determine whether the amount "raises a judicial eyebrow," as the Court said in *BMW v. Gore*. In that case, the Supreme Court said that courts should consider the "degree of reprehensibility of the manufacturer's conduct," the "reasonableness of the relationship of punitive award to compensatory award," and the typical fines charged in comparable civil and criminal cases. If a state law fines people $15,000 for criminal fraud, for example, then assessing millions in punitive damages in a civil product liability case seems unreasonable.[14]

Some states use formulas to calculate a reasonable amount. These can be based on the defendant's annual income or the profit the company made on the act in question. Some courts

QUOTABLE

George L. Priest, Professor of Law and Economics, Yale Law School

Our society is deeply committed to employing the force of government with reason and consistency. Discrepant punishments for the same act (or punishment in some but no punishment in others) or punishments disproportionate to the wrongfulness of the act are inconsistent with that commitment.

Source: George L. Priest, "Introduction: The Problem and Efforts to Understand It," in *Punitive Damages: How Juries Decide*, Chicago, Ill.: University of Chicago Press, 2002, p. 3.

must give written justifications for a punitive damages award as well as the amount. Requiring this kind of accountability in *every* court could improve the system.

Additionally, formulas and even caps can be set for awards. Standards might be twice the amount for economic and other non-economic losses, or a specific sum, whichever is greater. ATRA has suggested setting this amount at $250,000.[15] Maximum awards would be set lower for small businesses, since a single award can put them out of business. For small businesses, some observers have suggested a maximum of $250,000, with a limit of a single award to avoid double jeopardy. States that cap punitive damages at some multiple of the compensatory damage award include Colorado (multiple of one); Connecticut, North Dakota, and Oklahoma (multiple of two); Florida and Nevada (multiple of three); and New Jersey (multiple of five). Absolute dollar amounts are imposed in some places, including Virginia and Kansas. Other states look at the net worth or gross income of the defendant when limiting these awards.

Some states bar punitive damages entirely. As of 2008, the states of Washington, Louisiana, Massachusetts, Nebraska, and New Hampshire either banned or severely limited punitive awards. A few other states permit them only under special circumstances. In still other states, including Kansas, judges determine the amount of punitive damages, even when a jury has the role of determining liability, to prevent so-called "runaway jury" awards. Opponents challenged this practice in Kansas, saying that people are entitled to a trial by jury, but the law was upheld on the basis that punitive damages are not part of a jury trial.

A standard fee schedule offers another solution. In *Punitive Damages: How Juries Decide*, Cass R. Sunstein suggests replacing the jury's verdict with a system of civil fines based on a damage schedule set by specialists and overseen by officials. They would act in a way similar to those who enforce fines imposed by the Environmental Protection Agency (EPA), Federal Aviation Administration (FAA), and other government agencies.[16]

People who oppose setting limits claim that the number and amounts of punitive damages have declined during recent years. Such statistics, however, do not reflect the fact that many defendants settle their cases before trial for fear of a huge jury verdict. Most product liability cases are, in fact, settled without a trial. The possibility of large punitive damages has an impact far beyond the actual numbers of adjudicated cases.

Where should punitive damages should go after they are assessed? Some critics say these are actually fines, not compensation, so they should go to special funds that benefit specific causes or to the general public, not to plaintiffs and their attorneys. In many cases, millions of dollars go to one person or family, even though the company is being penalized for a product or practices that affected many people. This enriches a few victims

Suggested Standards from the Product Liability Reform Act of 1997

Under A, Title I: PRODUCT LIABILITY REFORM

8. Section 108: Uniform standards for award of punitive damages

Punitive damages may be awarded if a plaintiff proves, by "clear and convincing evidence," that his or her harm was caused by the defendant's "conscious, flagrant indifference to the safety of others."

Punitive damages may be awarded up to two times compensatory damages or $250,000 whichever is greater. The judge is permitted to award punitive damages beyond this limit after considering certain factors, but the judge cannot exceed the amount of the jury's original award.

When the defendant is a small business (or similar entity) with less than 25 full-time employees, punitive damages may not exceed $250,000 or two times compensatory damages, whichever is less. When a small business is the defendant, the judge is not permitted to award punitive damages above this limit as the judge may when a big business is the defendant.

Source: Product Liability Reform Act of 1997 (Passed by Congress; vetoed by President Bill Clinton).

and their attorneys while others receive nothing. For these reasons, some states require that a specified portion of punitive damages go to the state for use in public works.

Juries should follow clear guidelines and judges should scrutinize their decisions.

Can juries make logical and fair decisions about punitive damages? Investigations found that, despite good intentions, jurors often find this task confusing. One team of researchers wrote:

> Jurors do not have a clear idea about the meaning of different "points" on the scale of dollars; they do not know whether $200,000, or $1 million, or $5 million is the right punishment for a particular instance of serious corporate misconduct. Hence we observe considerable variability when jurors translate their shared intention to punish into a dollar award.[17]

Author and law professor Cass R. Sunstein has studied the ways in which juries make their decisions:

> We found that our mock juries had a very hard time arriving at consistent, predictable judgments when using the scale of dollars, even when their moral judgments are both consistent and predictable. We concluded from our research that a major source of this unpredictability comes from the fact that people do not know how to translate their moral judgment into dollar amounts.[18]

A research team working with Sunstein stated, "We find that juries do not carefully follow judicial instructions, and indeed that they are willing to ignore a large number of the legally necessary conditions for punitive damages verdicts."[19] Sunstein also found that jurors "used 'hindsight bias,' believing that what happened should have been foreseen, and they also penalized corporations that based their decisions on careful cost-benefit analysis. This point raises a number of interesting issues about how people think and what they find immoral."[20]

Realizing that judicial scrutiny is needed, appellate courts have, since the 1990s, been reversing more punitive damages awards. Through *remittitur*—the process by which a jury's verdict is reduced if a judge believes the damages award is excessive—courts can grant a defendant's request for a new trial or a reversal and remand the case unless the plaintiff accepts a reduced award.

Judges could assume the role of assessing punitive damages after a jury has determined liability by using guidelines decided on by elected members of the legislature. Judges are less likely to be emotional, since they are far more familiar with the kinds of accidents and injuries that come up in these cases. They also understand the tactics attorneys use to impress a jury. Juries, on the other hand, may be far less impartial. Research has shown that juries are inclined to favor plaintiffs, whom they see as suffering individuals, over corporations and businesses. Plaintiffs' attorneys can exploit an antibusiness bias to win high punitive damages awards.

European countries have recognized the pitfalls of letting juries set punitive damages awards. Most do not use juries for civil trials (or even in most criminal trials), fearing that the juries cannot be objective. In the United Kingdom, for example, juries are available for criminal cases but are limited to civil cases involving defamation of character, false imprisonment, and malicious prosecution.

Punitive damages do not necessarily make consumers safer.

Do laws that limit liability increase product safety? Two professors from Emory University, Paul H. Rubin and Joanna Shepherd, looked at the effects of tort reform on accidents involving products other than motor vehicles. After studying the accident rates from 1981 to 2000 in states that passed reform laws, they concluded that these reforms actually can save lives by leading to lower prices for medical products and safety equipment. Rubin wrote, "Overall, we found that the risk-reducing effects of tort reform greatly outweigh the risk-increasing effects. Tort reforms in the states from 1981–2000 have led to an estimated 14,222 fewer accidental deaths."[21]

Rubin also examined the impact of specific reforms, including those that deal with punitive damages. Statistics showed that limiting punitive damages correlated with lower accident rates: "Specifically, we found that caps on noneconomic damages, caps on punitive damages, a higher evidence standard for punitive damages, product liability reform, and prejudgment interest reform led to fewer accidental deaths."[22]

Summary

Punitive damages should be reserved for behavior that shows malice or extremely reckless conduct on the part of the manufacturer. Punitive damages awards result in too much "jackpot justice" and a "litigation lottery," in which a few claimants and their attorneys can make millions of dollars.

Plaintiffs' attorneys claim they fulfill an important role for the public by going after these companies, but attorneys (who are often eager to reap large punitive awards) were not elected or appointed to police the marketplace. Only legislators who are accountable to the public can view product liability cases objectively, without an eye on their own financial gain.

Recent rulings by the U.S. Supreme Court and new state laws highlight the need for reform in this area of the law. The United States should consider the benefits of the approach used in most European countries, which bans or limits punitive damages and does not let juries make these judgments. A better system is possible through a combination of laws, specific guidelines, and judicial overview.

Courts Should Have Discretion in Awarding Damages

I n 1994, Douglas Axen's doctor prescribed Cordarone for his heart condition. Within weeks, Axen became legally blind. As it turned out, this drug could cause permanent eye damage in some patients. While hearing the case of *Axen v. American Home Products Corp.*, the jury learned that the company had known about this side effect for at least eight years. The FDA had asked the company to warn people about the more serious hazards of the drug instead of just saying that Cordarone could cause milder side effects, such as possible inflammation of nerves in the eye. After reviewing an ad for Cordarone, the FDA wrote to American Home Products (AHP), complaining that "our cautions have been ignored. . . . The advertisement is clearly intended to minimize the hazards of the drug and emphasize the drug's efficacy."[1] After a Mayo Clinic study showed that Cordarone had caused blindness in some patients, a regulatory agency in Canada insisted that AHP change its warning label in that country. The company did not change its labels in the United States, however, nor did it inform the FDA about the Mayo study or the new label being used in Canada.

When the court awarded Mr. Axen $22 million in punitive damages, the company appealed that decision. The appeals court, however, refused to lower the punitive award because it concluded that AHP "deliberately placed misleading information on its packaging in order to preserve sales."[2] The court realized that the plaintiff had suffered a permanent injury. Moreover, this product had injured other people, yet the company failed to inform doctors and patients about all the risks. The court felt that punitive damages clearly were in order and that it had the discretion to administer justice.

Punitive damages have been available in cases of negligence, fraud, and strict liability in tort. Through the years, the standards for awarding punitive damages have included flagrant disregard, willful and wanton misconduct, fraud, and gross misconduct. The potential for large punitive awards has played a key role in removing hazardous products from the market and has deterred companies from selling potentially hazardous products.

Critics have tried to limit punitive damages or ban them altogether. To rally support, they present anecdotes and unusual situations that distort the truth and present negative views of courts, attorneys, and juries. A closer look shows that punitive damages are rare, smaller than people think, and well deserved. They promote safety and hold companies accountable for egregious behavior.

Critics exaggerate the number and amounts of punitive damages awards.

Media outlets tend to publicize cases with very high awards or unusual circumstances, such as the McDonald's coffee case. In addition, people often see reports of the initial jury award but almost never hear about the reduced awards. They also may never hear details of the case that convinced the jury punitive damages were justified. The facts show that courts do an effective and reasonable job in assessing punitive damages awards.

Punitive damages are rare. When Michael Rustad and Thomas Koenig looked at every product liability case in the United States from 1965 to 1990, they found that punitive damages were awarded in only 355 cases, and 95 of them involved the same product (asbestos). Punitive damages awards in non-asbestos cases actually declined from 1986 to 1990. After punitive damages were awarded, 22 percent (78) of the judgments were totally upheld on appeal while 25 percent either were reversed or wholly or partially remitted. The awards also were lower than people tend to think. In these thousands of cases, the median compensatory award was $500,000 and the median punitive award was $625,000. Punitive damages of $1 million or more were awarded in just 36 percent of the 355 cases.[3]

In another study, the RAND Institute for Civil Justice (ICJ) looked at tort cases in 15 U.S. jurisdictions from 1985 to 1994. Punitive damages were awarded in just 4 percent of those verdicts.[4] The U.S. Department of Justice studied cases in 75 of the nation's largest counties during 1996. They found that only 3 percent of the plaintiffs who won their cases received punitive damages and the median award was about $31,000.[5] A report released in 1997 showed that punitive damages were awarded in only 2.6 of all products liability verdicts.[6]

A 2005 report from the Bureau of Justice Statistics showed a downward trend both in the number of punitive damage awards and the amounts. The median final award in product liability cases, including the class-action asbestos cases, was $567,000.[7] This trend has continued. According to data compiled by Bloomberg News, the top 10 punitive damages awards against companies in 2008 totaled $960 million—30 percent lower than the total awarded in 2007 and 63 percent lower than in 2006. No billion-dollar verdicts have been awarded since 2003.[8] Legal experts David G. Owen and

Jerry Phillips have noted, "Studies reveal that most such awards are moderate in size and usually well deserved."[9]

Even when large judgments are awarded, they may be lowered by a higher court or by agreement between the parties. This has been especially true since the U.S. Supreme Court decision in *BMW v. Gore* in 1996. For example, in *Barnett v. la Societe Anonyme Turbomeca France*, a helicopter crashed due to a defect the manufacturer knew about but concealed. The jury awarded $175 million in punitive damages, yet the trial court cut that to $87.5 million and the appellate court further reduced it to $26.5 million.[10] In the famous "Pinto cases" (see below), the original award for punitive damages was $125 million; in the end, the plaintiff collected much less: $3.5 million.[11]

The public hears less about cases in which injured victims collect far too little. For example, U.S. military veterans sued for damages from ailments they attribute to their exposure to Agent Orange, an herbicide used to defoliate jungle areas during the Vietnam War. This class-action suit yielded an award of $180 million, a record at that time, yet each claimant received only $12,000. Product liability expert W. Kip Viscusi points out that this amount of money "for injuries as severe as terminal cancer and genetic damage does not qualify as a windfall gain."[12] As for people who die from their injuries, Viscusi writes, "Victims of fatal product injuries certainly do not profit from an overly generous products liability system. Their families receive compensation usually based on the economic value of lost earnings less the share of these earnings that would have been spent to provide for the deceased."[13]

The threat of punitive damages helps to deter misconduct and to promote safer products.

Punitive damages give manufacturers a compelling reason to make safe products and to provide accurate warnings and instructions; they also deter companies from releasing products (such as chemicals or medicines) with undetermined long-term effects or side effects. Pharmaceutical companies know the consequences of providing false information about their products. Punitive damages have been awarded when these companies submitted false or misleading data to the FDA in order to obtain approval for drugs that later proved hazardous.

In numerous cases, lawsuits involving punitive damages awards have caused companies to pull unsafe products off the market. These include the Ford Pinto, the Dalkon shield, highly flammable children's pajamas, super-absorbent tampons linked to toxic shock syndrome, tires made from poor quality rubber that could cause the tread to separate, football helmets that did not protect high school athletes from brain injury, and various prescription drugs.

If punitive damages were limited or unavailable, companies might decide that the financial risk of selling a potentially hazardous product is small, compared with the profits. Companies often use a cost-benefit analysis when they consider alternative designs and launch new products. If they are not liable for unpredictable punitive damages, they might choose a design that is less safe but cheaper, because the cost of lawsuits will be lower than the cost of making the product safer.

The Ford Pinto automobile cases show how this works. The Pinto—an inexpensive subcompact car made by Ford in the 1970s—could explode when hit from the rear, where the fuel tank was located, and passengers died or were severely injured during such crashes. The court in *Grimshaw v. Ford Motor Company* noted the deterrence benefits of punitive damages when it said, "The manufacturer may find it more profitable to treat compensatory damages as a part of the cost of doing business rather than to remedy the defect. . . . Punitive damages thus remain as the most effective remedy for consumer protection against defectively designed mass-produced articles."[14]

Because manufacturers can keep defective products out of the marketplace, courts have been willing to impose extra damages for

A photo of a 1973 Ford Pinto sedan after it was wrecked by a collision with a 1972 Chevrolet van. This image was shown in February 1980 as part of the evidence at a Ford Pinto trial in Winamac, Indiana.

conduct that puts people at risk. This is especially true when the cost of making the product safer or of issuing adequate warnings is minimal. For example, an Ohio court awarded punitive damages when a company that made color TV sets used a high-voltage transformer that was known to cause fires. The cost of fixing the problem would have been just one dollar per set.[15] Punitive damages also were awarded after a chemical preservative manufacturer failed to warn users that inhalation could cause death, although the manufacturer knew about nine deaths that had occurred this way. The warning mentioned only irritation, burns, and allergic reactions.

Some people suggest that adhering to federal standards should shield people from punitive damages, but this kind of compliance does not guarantee a safe product. Consider the FDA, for example. In some cases, companies gave the FDA inaccurate or incomplete information in order to gain approval. Medications and medical devices approved by the FDA have contained safety defects, yet manufacturers downplayed the risks or failed to mention them. The Bjork-Shiley heart valve received FDA approval but was later found to be unsafe. When law professor Lucinda Finley testified before Congress about cases like these, she asked:

> Why should a manufacturer of any sort of product whose conduct meets the standard of conscious and flagrant disregard for human safety be insulated from punitive damages simply because a regulatory agency, which may or may not have adequate enforcement resources or, depending on the political times, a strong commitment to enforcement, has previously approved the device?[16]

While the regulatory process is going on, more people might be injured. The potential for awards in court, however, encourages victims to come forward and provides incentives for skilled attorneys to press their cases in court, which in turn brings unsafe products to people's attention. Punitive awards show manufacturers they cannot profit from misconduct by hitting the manufacturers in the pocketbook.

Assessing damages also adds fairness in the overall economy. It reduces the competitive edge a company might gain when it saves money by producing less safe goods. If the makers of unsafe products must pay extra for their misdeeds, their more conscientious competitors will have a more level playing field.

Juries can make sound judgments regarding punitive damages awards.

Research has shown that jury-rendered punitive damages are justified. In the vast majority of cases, defendants who receive punitive damages suffered extensive injuries or death. Most cases in which juries award punitive damages also involve one or more kinds of misbehavior on the part of manufacturers. These include fraud, a knowing violation of safety standards, failure to adequately test for safety, and failure to design in ways that avoid known dangers. They also may have failed to warn of known dangers or to fix defects that become apparent after the product is sold. In the case of the Dalkon shield contraceptive, critics claim the manufacturer knew this device could cause infection in a woman's womb and other serious problems and that a change in the design, involving different materials in the tail string, could have reduced that risk.[17]

Well-known cases have been distorted to present a negative view of punitive damages. Much was made of the jury award in the McDonald's coffee case, with many tort reform advocates arguing the jury did not use common sense. They failed to note that the jury heard testimony showing that McDonald's earned about $2.7 million every two days from coffee sales. The jurors used that information to calculate punitive damages.[18]

Critics say that noneconomic damages are too subjective and cannot be calculated clearly. Yet in many cases, the emotional and social effects of injuries are even more devastating than the loss of income or medical costs that are covered through compensatory damages. In some cases, such as a birth-control device that leads to permanent infertility, the medical condition (an infection) may require only brief treatment, while the impact of infertility lasts a lifetime and affects the entire family. Though money cannot remove emotional suffering or chronic pain, nor can it make up for the loss of a limb or infertility, it can give injured parties options they would not have otherwise. It can help them to obtain better medical treatments, to further their education, to hire healthcare aides, and/or to buy special equipment to improve their quality of life.

While some argue that juries are less capable of objectivity than judges, this line of reasoning ignores the fact that many judges are elected and might be inclined to make decisions that please their constituents. Other judges are political appointees, so their decisions may reflect their parties' attitudes. A judge also is just one person, while a jury verdict requires a group consensus. In some states, laws granting judges the option to determine punitive damages have been struck down on constitutional grounds. The Ohio court made that finding, based on the right to a jury trial. As for the idea that juries are less objective and more prone to side with plaintiffs, statistics gathered in 1996 showed that judges were more likely than juries to award punitive damages (in 8 percent of cases, versus 3 percent for juries).[19]

Statistics also show that the idea of "runaway juries" is largely false. In another 1996 study (conducted by two professors from Cornell University and three analysts from the National Center for State Courts, an independent research group based in Virginia), researchers looked at 8,724 civil trials and found that judges and juries in product liability cases awarded punitive damages at about the same rate, with judges awarding slightly more.[20]

Federal courts uphold the constitutionality of punitive damages and jury discretion.

Through the years, people have challenged punitive damages in court, sometimes by arguing that such damages should be banned under the Eighth and Fourteenth amendments. The U.S. Supreme Court itself has considered various challenges to the amounts of awards as well as the legitimacy of punitive damages themselves. The Court continues to say punitive damages are permissible.

In 1984, the U.S. Supreme Court noted: "Punitive damages have long been a part of traditional state tort law."[21] In 1763, English courts, upon which American courts were modeled, decided that a jury had the right to award punitive (also called "exemplary") damages. Lord Chief Justice Pratt explained that these damages were "a punishment to the guilty, to deter from any such proceeding for the future, and as a proof of the detestation of the jury to the action itself."[22] In the United States, the first punitive damages were awarded in 1784.

In an 1851 case, the U.S. Supreme Court said that both statute and common law provided a basis for punitive damages and that such damages could "properly be termed exemplary or vindictive rather than compensatory" and that a jury had the discretion to make this determination based "on the peculiar circumstances of each case."[23] The decision said:

> It is a well-established principle of the common law, that in actions of trespass and all actions on the case for torts, a jury may inflict what are called exemplary, punitive, or vindictive damages upon a defendant, having in view the enormity of his offense rather than the measure of compensation to the plaintiff. . . . By the common as well as by statute law, men are often punished for aggravated misconduct or lawless acts, by means of a civil action, and the damages, inflicted by way of penalty or punishment, given to the party injured.[24]

The Court further stated, "This has been always left to the discretion of the jury, as the degree of punishment to be thus inflicted must depend on the peculiar circumstances of each case."[25]

In a 1989 case, the Supreme Court rejected the argument that punitive damages awards violate the Excessive Fines Clause of the Eighth Amendment. The Court noted that the word "fine" referred to a payment to a sovereign, and that the amendment did not limit punitive damages in actions between private parties, although it did limit the government's ability to punish and deter individuals. The Court found "no basis for concluding that the Excessive Fines Clause operates to limit the ability of a civil jury to award punitive damages."[26] Though this was not a product liability case, the Court's reading of the Eighth Amendment still applies.

An appeals court in Oregon also looked at the Eighth Amendment when a company argued that a punitive damages award of $20 million was an excessive fine because the state of Oregon receives a portion of punitive damages awards in product liability cases. In *Axen v. American Home Products Corp.*, the court said that the Eighth Amendment is not implicated in "a civil case in which the government has no *prosecutorial* role."[27]

Two years later, in *Pacific Mutual Life Insurance Co. v. Haslip*, the U.S. Supreme Court rejected the argument that punitive damages violate the Due Process Clause of the Constitution. The Court did find that the clause applies to punitive damages awards between private litigants but said the state court in this case did not violate the defendant's rights. The Court also did not set rigid rules for determining amounts, though it said that a punitive award four times the amount of compensatory damages "might be close to the line of constitutional impropriety."[28] Even so, the Court did not overturn a punitive damages decision in a fraud case that it heard in 1993. The punitive award was $10 million, as compared to compensatory damages of only $19,000.[29]

In 1996, in the case of *BMW v. Gore*, the Court did conclude that the amount of punitive damages was excessive and offered guidelines (though not a rigid formula) for determining reasonable damages. Four out of nine justices dissented. In her dissent, Justice Ruth Bader Ginsburg, joined by Chief Justice William H. Rehnquist, wrote that the Court "unnecessarily and unwisely ventures into territory traditionally within the states' domain, and does so in the face of reform measures recently adopted or currently under consideration in legislative arenas."[30]

In the case of *State Farm Mutual Auto Ins. Co. v. Campbell*, Supreme Court Justice Anthony Kennedy wrote that "there are no rigid benchmarks" and so larger ratios in damages (comparative and punitive) can be acceptable "where a particularly egregious act has resulted in only a small amount of economic damages."[31]

Summary

For more than 200 years, America's legal system and common laws have developed in ways that protect average citizens. Victims of product injuries need not be wealthy or powerful to get their day in court. The potential for punitive damages makes this more possible, since highly qualified attorneys have incentives to take such cases. It also means that victims can receive more compensation for the full range of their injuries.

Though many people think otherwise, large punitive awards have been rare and are becoming rarer. Many are lowered after trial. Despite this, critics continue to push for limits that favor defendants. Some recent state legislation limiting punitive damages makes the civil justice system less fair and less available to injured parties. Attorney Grant Woods writes, "When the threat of punitives was there, the courthouse was a level playing field. Now the threat of consequence isn't there for billion-dollar corporations."[32]

Punitive damages force companies to recognize the social and emotional costs of the harm they caused. History shows that many unsafe products remained on the market until companies faced lawsuits and punitive damages. The legal system must act when regulations and market forces do not motivate businesses to reduce risks and protect victims.

Debates Go On

In 1999, Mitchell and Hilda Bankston found out they were being sued. At the time, the couple owned and ran the Bankston Drugstore in Fayette, Mississippi, a family business they started in 1971. Theirs also was the only pharmacy in Jefferson County. The Bankstons had been named as defendants in a class-action product liability lawsuit filed on behalf of people who had taken a drug called Fen-Phen. Through the years, the Bankston's pharmacy had filled doctors' prescriptions for Fen-Phen, which the FDA had approved for weight loss. The company that made Fen-Phen was located in New Jersey, but the plaintiffs' attorneys knew they could have the case tried in Jefferson County if the Bankstons were codefendants. This county was known for its tendency to rule in favor of plaintiffs in product liability cases.

As a result of the lawsuit, more than 100 Fen-Phen customers sued the Bankstons. Three weeks after the suit was filed, 58-year-old Mitchell Bankston, who had been in good health, died of a massive heart attack. Hilda Bankston sold the pharmacy in 2000 but had to deal with these lawsuits for years afterward. In 2004, she wrote that she had spent "countless hours" gathering documents and records for plaintiffs' attorneys and "was dragged into court on numerous occasions to testify. . . . I still get named as a defendant time and again."[1]

Should such a small business face legal action for selling drugs or medical devices that were approved by the FDA and prescribed by a doctor? Many people agreed that Fen-Phen posed risks to consumers and should have been removed from the market. They also thought the manufacturer should be held liable. But critics said it was unfair to include people like the Bankstons in such lawsuits. The case prompted heated debates about class-action suits and the ability to choose a favorable jurisdiction—called *forum shopping*—by naming defendants who have even a remote connection to the case.

Class-Action Reform

In a class-action lawsuit, people join together in one legal case against the defendant(s). Combining claims can be more efficient than conducting numerous similar lawsuits. In some cases, the amounts of money involved per case also might be too small to justify a lawsuit unless they are combined. Class-action suits also can foster a more consistent result with similar remedies for all plaintiffs.

Critics, however, have complained about some aspects of these cases, including forum shopping and the naming of defendants with weak connections to the case. They also express concerns about the way fees are collected and distributed. Sometimes members of the class action receive small amounts or even just coupons or vouchers instead of money.

After a decade of debate, Congress passed the Class Action Fairness Act of 2005. As this law was being debated, Senator Dianne Feinstein (D-California) introduced a letter she received from Hilda Bankston, which said in part:

> This lawsuit frenzy has hurt my family and my community. Businesses will no longer locate in Jefferson County because of fear of litigation. The county's reputation has driven liability insurance rates through the roof. . . . No small business should have to endure the nightmares I have experienced. I'm not a lawyer, but to me, something is wrong with our legal system when innocent bystanders are little more than pawns for lawyers seeking to win the "jackpot" in Jefferson County—or any other county in the United States where lawsuits are "big business."[2]

The Class Action Fairness Act of 2005 allows federal courts to hear cases involving plaintiffs and defendants from different states in suits that meet certain specifications. Senator Feinstein said, "The Framers of the Constitution wanted Federal courts to settle disputes between citizens of different States. . . . The Constitution itself states that the Federal judicial power 'shall extend . . . to controversies between citizens of different States.'"[3] It limits forum shopping by letting defendants remove suits to federal courts if minimal diversity exists, if the class involves more than 100 people, and/or if the total amount in contention is over $5 million. The act does make two exceptions: A federal court can decline jurisdiction over a class-action suit when more than one-third but less than two-thirds of the proposed class members and primary defendants are citizens of the forum state based on certain factors. If, for example, more than two-thirds of the plaintiffs are from the forum state or the principal injuries occurred in the forum state, the federal court must decline to hear it.

The act also provides more federal scrutiny and procedures to review class-action settlements. It changes the rules for evaluating settlements in which class members receive coupons, not cash. The court must hold a hearing and make a written finding that the coupon settlement is "fair, reasonable, and adequate for class members." In the case of unclaimed coupons, the court may require that a portion of their value be given to one or more charitable or governmental organizations. (The value cannot be included in calculating attorneys' fees.) The act also reduces attorneys' fees if they are deemed excessive compared to what class members received.

President George W. Bush said it would help to end "junk lawsuits" and protect small businesses. The president noted that class-action lawsuits can serve useful purposes but "can also be manipulated for personal gain" and noted the law would "prevent trial lawyers from shopping around for friendly local venues" and "keep out-of-state businesses, workers and shareholders from being dragged before unfriendly local juries."[4]

Critics have called the act unfair and even unconstitutional because it poses barriers to holding businesses accountable for hazardous products. Some analysts note that the ability of federal judges to overturn settlements delays the judicial process, forcing people to start over. Further delays can occur as federal courts strain to keep up with new cases.

Mass Torts

Recent large-scale class-action lawsuits involving products have been called *mass torts*. Traditionally, product liability suits required proof that individuals suffered from injury or other harm from a specific product that came from a specific source. Before the 1970s, this prevented suits with large groups of plaintiffs who used products made by more than one defendant, often over a period of years. For example, courts were unwilling to award money to individual smokers who smoked various kinds of cigarettes over the years, and this posed a barrier in tobacco liability cases.

Attorneys began using statistical projections to show what likely harm would result from years of product sales and market shares. This strategy was used to sue tobacco companies on a large scale. Attorneys representing states as their plaintiffs said tobacco sellers should compensate the states for the costs of caring for sick smokers through the Medicaid public health insurance program. Since it is not possible to prove which cigarette caused which health problems or even if smoking is the sole cause of these problems, the attorneys presented statistics about the healthcare costs associated with smoking. In view of these problems with "cause and effect," attorneys relied on warning defects, saying that tobacco companies knew the dangers of smoking decades before they acknowledged these dangers on their warning labels.

Soon states across the nation were suing the tobacco companies. State legislatures abolished the ways in which tobacco companies had defended themselves against these kinds of cases in the past. After several years of litigation, the tobacco companies agreed to pay the states $246 billion—an unprecedented award for a product liability case.

People opposed to these lawsuits say that smokers are responsible for health problems resulting from tobacco use because they knew or should have known the hazards of smoking. Supporters, however, counter that most smokers begin in their teens and then become addicted to smoking before they have the judgment of an adult. Because the tobacco companies knew about these hazards but kept them from the public, they should be held liable.

The retroactive nature of these suits has come under fire, since companies are held liable for the costs of doing business many years ago. In those days, companies did not know they would face these future legal judgments, so they did not set the funds aside. Citing these kinds of problems, product liability expert W. Kip Viscusi says tort liability does not work well in these kinds of cases because mass torts are "not simply scaled-up versions of manufacturing defect cases. Rather, they pose a new class of products liability issues."[5] Insurers and companies find themselves overwhelmed and even go bankrupt before they can pay every victim. Such liability does not promote compensation or the deterrence of dangerous products.

Similar issues arise in the mass tort cases involving environmental toxins such as asbestos. The causes of disease can be complex and hard to pinpoint. A person's exposure to many things in many places, along with the person's own health habits, can play a role in various diseases. People are not always sure which manufacturer made the product or how long ago it was made. Some plaintiffs were exposed to asbestos in the military, at a job, in various buildings, or in other places. Often, there is a long time period between exposure to the substance and the development of a disease.

The resulting scientific debates that take place in the courtroom can confuse juries and even judges. Though scientific relationships can be shown, this is not the same as proof with clear cause and effect. Outcomes in these cases have varied, sometimes widely, depending on where they were heard and who made the decision.

The role of the lawyers and the high fees they collect in mass tort cases also is a source of complaint. Catherine Crier writes:

> We are permitting the plaintiffs' bar to determine state and national policy. Its motives are no purer than those of corporate special interest groups, and its tactics are the same. These legal groups contribute millions of dollars to those officials who can assist in their schemes, and billions are returned back to them as contingency fees.[6]

Critics also express concerns about the enormous attorneys' fees and how state officials chose those attorneys. In *The Rule of Lawyers*, Walter K. Olson writes:

> Who got picked for these lucrative deals? In most big states, attorneys general selected the outside counsel

with a minimum of competitive bidding, publicity, or other formalities. Again and again they picked lawyers who were among their own biggest campaign donors or were strongly tied in other ways to the state's political establishment.[7]

Some suggest that when lawyers from private practices are hired to represent a state, a competitive bidding process should be used. States have since passed laws that require such bidding. States also may require attorneys to keep time sheets showing the actual time they spent on the case. These measures do not go far enough, however, for those who say attorneys in these cases should not be paid on a contingency basis at all.

Aside from attorneys' contingent fees, these mass tort cases have had high transaction cases overall. By 2000, about $54 billion had been spent to resolve the asbestos cases.[8] D. Alan Rudlin says that the process for resolving the claims has been "remarkably inefficient" and that "61 percent has gone to defense and claimants' 'transaction costs' (principally, attorneys' fees)."[9]

Critics worry that tobacco lawsuits opened the door for lawsuits targeting people who sell other potentially dangerous products, including foods high in sugar and fat, alcoholic beverages, and guns. Plaintiffs could again claim that someone should pay for the healthcare and social costs associated with these items. Food companies could be sued for states' costs of treating people who have heart attacks and other diseases related to obesity. In the case of alcohol, manufacturers and sellers might be sued for all drunk-driving accidents and crimes involving alcohol.

Since 2000, several companies have been forced to defend lawsuits brought by people who said their foods were unhealthy and caused them to gain too much weight. In New York in 2002, a group of teenagers filed a lawsuit against McDonald's, alleging the restaurants were negligent because they sold foods high in salt, fat, and sugar. The suit was dismissed for being not clear or specific enough, so the attorneys filed a new suit alleging "deceptive practices" in the way McDonald's promoted and advertised certain foods. This case also was dismissed, since the court said the plaintiffs could not prove that McDonald's foods were the direct cause of their obesity and related health problems. Although these cases did not succeed, more legal showdowns over food seem likely.

At the same time, class-action suits have been filed against gun manufacturers, prompting critics to say lawyers are trying to achieve gun regulation through litigation. By suing gun manufacturers for crimes committed with guns, the lawyers can achieve stricter gun control and manage to "regulate" the firearms industry without a gun-control law from Congress.

Personal Responsibility in Food Consumption Act of 2005 (proposed legislation)

From SEC. 2. FINDINGS; PURPOSE.:
(a) FINDINGS.—Congress finds that—
(1) the food and beverage industries are a significant part of our national economy;
(2) the activities of manufacturers and sellers of foods and beverages substantially affect interstate and foreign commerce;
(3) a person's weight gain, obesity, or a health condition associated with a person's weight gain or obesity is based on a multitude of factors, including genetic factors and the lifestyle and physical fitness decisions of individuals, such that a person's weight gain, obesity, or a health condition associated with a person's weight gain or obesity cannot be attributed to the consumption of any specific food or beverage; and
(4) because fostering a culture of acceptance of personal responsibility is one of the most important ways to promote a healthier society, lawsuits seeking to blame individual food and beverage providers for a person's weight gain, obesity, or a health condition associated with a person's weight gain or obesity are not only legally frivolous and economically damaging, but also harmful to a healthy America.

Source: H.R. 554, Report No. 109—130, 109th Congress, 1st Session, http://thomas.loc.gov/home/gpoxmlc109/h554_rh.xml.

What about people who have been exposed to a hazard-ous substance but have no disease? In the asbestos cases, many people who are receiving money have no proven disease as a result of their exposure. Some have pleural changes—changes that can be detected in their lung tissue—but there is no proof asbestos caused the changes, since many of these people also are smokers. Some people argue that it is necessary to compen-sate these people now, since there is a good chance they might develop a disease later on and by then, the money for a settle-ment might be gone. Catherine Crier writes, "Many people truly suffering from asbestos exposure may never recover a dime as company after company goes belly up paying plaintiffs with no apparent injury."[10]

Successor Liability

Under successor liability laws, companies can be liable for the actions of their predecessor company or companies. This hap-pened to Crown Cork & Seal Company. The Philadelphia-based company, founded in the 1890s by the man who invented the bottle cap, operated a successful beverage and food packaging business. Although Crown had never made, sold, marketed, or distributed any asbestos products, it became a defendant in asbestos lawsuits because it had purchased Mundet Cork, a competitor bottle-cap company, in 1963 for $7 million. That company shut down its small asbestos operation within 93 days after Crown bought Mundet.[11] Starting in the 1960s, more than 300,000 claims were filed against Crown Cork & Seal. By December 2001, the company had paid out more than $535 mil-lion.[12] In 2002, a federal court granted the company's motion to dismiss 376 remaining asbestos claims against Crown Cork, based on new state legislation passed in 2001 that said a succes-sor company's liability in asbestos cases would be limited to the value of the company that had asbestos-related activities at the time the successor company bought it.

Critics say that successor liability hurts the general economy and costs many American jobs. Companies have gone bankrupt paying claims related to businesses they bought. State legislators have pointed out that if their states maintain such laws, companies may avoid operating in their states, causing the loss of jobs and taxes. Supporters, however, say these laws offer victims a source of compensation for their injuries. They point out that companies can offset their losses by gaining a federal tax deduction, as well as by spreading the costs of insurance among their customers.

Joint and Several Liability

Many jurisdictions apply joint and several liability in product cases. This theory of recovery means that multiple defendants in the lawsuit can be liable for some or all of the plaintiff's damages, regardless of their degree of fault or responsibility. In some cases, the party with the least or even a scanty degree of fault (for example, 1 percent) can be stuck with the entire judgment if none of the other defendants have resources. A poor defendant who is responsible for most of the injury could pay nothing. Plaintiffs also can collect large sums from a defendant who is less responsible for their injuries than they are. For this reason, joint liability is sometimes called the *deep pocket rule*.

Reformers suggest replacing joint liability with proportionate liability so people would pay only to the extent they are responsible for the injury. Others disagree and say joint liability is essential so that damages are always covered. Some states, however, have modified the way they apply joint liability: Some ban it except in cases of intentional acts or in specific classes of offenses (for example, dumping hazardous waste products). In New York, when a defendant is less than 50 percent at fault, that party is not subject to joint and several liability. In California, joint and several liability is applied to economic damages, but damages for pain and suffering are assessed based on fault.

Scientific Testimony

People are concerned about the quality of evidence in product liability cases, especially when it involves highly technical or scientific material. In some cases, this results in a "battle of the experts," where the most charismatic or convincing expert can win, whether or not that person has more actual facts or more credible information than the opposition. Critics say "junk science" prevails in some cases, such as the silicone breast implant controversy of recent decades.

During the 1980s and 1990s, tens of thousands of women sued Dow Corning, claiming that the silicone in their implants caused health problems, including autoimmune diseases, neurological problems, and breast cancer. Many courts found in favor of the plaintiffs, though Dow Corning said no scientific studies found a clear link between silicone implants and these health problems. The company filed for bankruptcy in 1995 after paying out billions of dollars in compensatory and punitive damages for the lawsuits. In the meantime, studies conducted by the Mayo Clinic, the American College of Rheumatology, the Harvard Nurses Epidemiology Study, and others concluded that women with silicone breast implants were not at higher risk for these diseases than other women.[13]

Critics say juries frequently do not have the needed expertise to evaluate scientific testimony, especially when sorting out complex issues of cause and effect. They also warn that when junk science is allowed in the courtroom, manufacturers will hesitate to make potentially useful products, for fear they will be blamed for effects their products did not cause.

What kind of scientific evidence should be allowed in court? In the 1993 case of *Daubert v. Merrell Dow Pharmaceuticals, Inc.*, parents sued the manufacturer of Bendectin, claiming that their two children were born with birth defects because the mother took this drug to relieve nausea during pregnancy. The two sides disagreed about the credibility of expert testimony in the case. The U.S. Supreme Court said federal trial judges should aim to prevent unreliable scientific testimony from being presented in court. Such testimony should be both relevant and reliable, said the Court. It offered five standards that judges can use to decide what will be admissible in court. For example, the judge can consider whether the scientific technique in question has been tested in field conditions as well as in a laboratory.[14]

Four years later, in *General Electric Co. v. Joiner*, the Court affirmed this opinion. It said that the lower court had a right to determine whether or not expert testimony in the case rose above the level of "subjective belief or unsupported speculation." Writing for a unanimous Court, Chief Justice Rehnquist said, "We . . . hold that, because it was within the District Court's discretion to conclude that the studies upon which the experts relied were not sufficient . . . to support their conclusions that Joiner's exposure to PCBs contributed to his cancer, the District Court did not abuse its discretion in excluding their testimony."[15] Supporters praise these Court decisions as important reforms in the tort system.

Other nations have sought ways to ensure the quality of scientific evidence in court. In the UK, critics have said that even judges cannot be expected to know enough to evaluate all the potential expert testimony. In 2005, the United Kingdom's House of Commons Science and Technology suggested that a Forensic Science Advisory Panel be set up to deal with these matters.

Statutes of Limitations and Repose

In some cases, companies have been sued for products they made 50 years ago or more. Examples include elevators, which can last for more than 100 years. People have sued elevator makers when they tripped on unleveled elevators or were injured from a door closing or opening. An attorney for a U.S. elevator supplier explained:

> [I]t is not unusual for manufacturers to be sued for equipment that has been in service for more than 70 years. . . . Typically, alleged accidents happen without any witnesses or other clear evidence that an accident has occurred. In nearly one-third of the accidents, our

first notice that an accident may have taken place will come two or three years after the accident, when we are served with a summons and complaint.[16]

In other cases, lawsuits claim that the products are faulty because they do not include improvements or new safety features that came along after the products were made. Manufacturers say they should not be required to modify all of their old products with new safety features in order to escape the threat of lawsuits. They also claim it is unfair to ask that they notify everyone who bought an older product each time the company makes a newer model. Such debates relate to the discussion of "state-of-the art" products discussed in the chapter on strict liability.

Some states have passed laws that may set a limit on how old a product may be and/or the amount of time after an injury during which victims can bring a lawsuit. These help to avoid the unpredictability and confusion that can stem from unlimited liability. In fashioning these laws, states can make exceptions for special circumstances, including negligence or fault.

Double Compensation (Collateral Source Issues)

Most jurisdictions do not consider health insurance or disability payouts when they award damages in a product liability lawsuit. Courts are not allowed to deduct these when they calculate damages. Critics say that because private or public health insurance often covers injuries, lawsuit judgments should not duplicate those payments. Others disagree, arguing that deducting these amounts would penalize those who prepare in case of a disaster. This approach also would let manufacturers benefit from something the plaintiffs took care to do on their own.

State laws that allow juries to deduct these amounts have been challenged in court. For instance, Kansas state legislators passed a law allowing evidence of other payments for the injury to be deducted from a judgment. The state's supreme court said this was unconstitutional because it violated the equal protection guarantees by discriminating against a certain class of plaintiffs, namely people with insurance.

Criticizing Attorneys

Critics say some attorneys take cases of little merit, knowing they can at least force a settlement out of court, and note that contingent fees encourage lawsuits, especially mass torts and class-action suits. Other nations do not use this system; people in those countries pay attorneys whether they win or lose. Reformers have proposed caps on fees and sliding scales where the rates go lower as the amount of a judgment goes higher. Supporters, however, point out that many clients could not afford to hire an attorney if they had to pay their own expenses out-of-pocket. Attorneys put in time and incur costs and often go unpaid.

Are contingent fees likely to disappear? Many people say this will not happen because of powerful lobbying efforts and campaign contributions by organized trial attorneys. In its Washington "Power 25" surveys, *Fortune* found that the American Trial Lawyers Association (ATLA) ranks as the fifth most powerful lobbying group in Washington, D.C.[17] One of their main goals is to prevent tort reform that would limit lawsuits and damage awards in civil cases. Walter K. Olson notes that American lawyers have "far more power" than attorneys in other countries, as well as less supervision.[18] An independent watchdog agency is one answer, Olson says, that could make activities more transparent.

Making Informed Decisions?

As history shows, debates about product liability law can be heated as people advocate their positions and cite studies and statistics to support them. Critics note, however, that the opposing sides could all use more unbiased and accurate information. People question the reliability of the information used for making decisions. This is especially true in areas that are hard to measure, such as the social consequences of product liability laws.

As previous chapters have shown, each side worries that their opponents form conclusions based on anecdotes, half-truths, mistruths, urban legends, bizarre cases, or speculation. John Cochran writes:

> No one routinely collects detailed comprehensive information on insurance claims, so it is not at all clear what's driving costs throughout the system. Nor is there national data on out-of-court settlements, which are by far the majority of payouts, since only a small fraction of claims ever end up in court—and even smaller fraction of those ever go to trial.[19]

THE LETTER OF THE LAW

Sanctions for Attorneys

Under Rule 11, Federal Rules of Civil Procedure, federal judges can sanction attorneys for filing complaints in federal court that are seen as frivolous or without merit. Critics say that this is not used often enough. The rule provides, in part:

(b) Representations to the Court.

By presenting to the court a pleading, written motion, or other paper—whether by signing, filing, submitting, or later advocating it—an attorney or unrepresented party certifies that to the best of the person's knowledge, information, and belief, formed after an inquiry reasonable under the circumstances:

(1) it is not being presented for any improper purpose, such as to harass, cause unnecessary delay, or needlessly increase the cost of litigation;

(2) the claims, defenses, and other legal contentions are warranted by existing law or by a nonfrivolous argument for extending, modifying, or reversing existing law or for establishing new law;

(3) the factual contentions have evidentiary support or, if specifically so identified, will likely have evidentiary support after a reasonable opportunity for further investigation or discovery; and

(4) the denials of factual contentions are warranted on the evidence or, if specifically so identified, are reasonably based on belief or a lack of information.

Source: http://msgre2.people.wm.edu/FRCP8(d).html.

People also may generalize when they talk about the impact of product liability. For example, in the area of product development, litigation does not seem to affect all industries in the same way. When they studied innovation, Huber and Litan noted "devastating effects" on general aviation but not much of an impact in chemicals.[20]

As with any controversy, it is important to know where information came from, how it was gathered, and who did the gathering. John Cochran comments, "The most striking thing about the entire debate—which pits businesses and insurance companies against lawyers and consumer advocates—is how little either side really knows about the system whose future they are debating with such passion and conviction."[21]

Summary

In recent years, debates over class-action suits and mass tort actions have led to new laws at the state and federal level. Reform advocates have praised measures that require a higher standard of proof and set more limits on damages and attorney's fees. They favor laws that would set firm statutes of repose and limitation, require more care and responsibility on the part of product users, and reduce the costs of doing business. Consumer advocates and trial lawyers, however, express concerns that these measures will make it harder for injured people to have their day in court. They worry that more courts will move away from the standard of strict liability and require less from manufacturers in terms of care and warning labels. They believe that product liability cases help make products safer and compensate injured victims.

Courts continue working to balance the competing rights of plaintiffs and defendants in product liability cases. State and federal legislatures also play a role as these laws evolve. Analysts say that more accurate and unbiased information is essential for making the most effective decisions.

Beginning Legal Research

The goals of each book in the Point/Counterpoint series are not only to give the reader a basic introduction to a controversial issue affecting society, but also to encourage the reader to explore the issue more fully. This Appendix is meant to serve as a guide to the reader in researching the current state of the law as well as exploring some of the public policy arguments as to why existing laws should be changed or new laws are needed.

Although some sources of law can be found primarily in law libraries, legal research has become much faster and more accessible with the advent of the Internet. This Appendix discusses some of the best starting points for free access to laws and court decisions, but surfing the Web will uncover endless additional sources of information. Before you can research the law, however, you must have a basic understanding of the American legal system.

The most important source of law in the United States is the Constitution. Originally enacted in 1787, the Constitution outlines the structure of our federal government, as well as setting limits on the types of laws that the federal government and state governments can enact. Through the centuries, a number of amendments have added to or changed the Constitution, most notably the first 10 amendments, which collectively are known as the "Bill of Rights" and which guarantee important civil liberties.

Reading the plain text of the Constitution provides little information. For example, the Constitution prohibits "unreasonable searches and seizures" by the police. To understand concepts in the Constitution, it is necessary to look to the decisions of the U.S. Supreme Court, which has the ultimate authority in interpreting the meaning of the Constitution. For example, the U.S. Supreme Court's 2001 decision in *Kyllo v. United States* held that scanning the outside of a person's house using a heat sensor to determine whether the person is growing marijuana is an unreasonable search—if it is done without first getting a search warrant from a judge. Each state also has its own constitution and a supreme court that is the ultimate authority on its meaning.

Also important are the written laws, or "statutes," passed by the U.S. Congress and the individual state legislatures. As with constitutional provisions, the U.S. Supreme Court and the state supreme courts are the ultimate authorities in interpreting the meaning of federal and state laws, respectively. However, the U.S. Supreme Court might find that a state law violates the U.S. Constitution, and a state supreme court might find that a state law violates either the state or U.S. Constitution.

Not every controversy reaches either the U.S. Supreme Court or the state supreme courts, however. Therefore, the decisions of other courts are also important. Trial courts hear evidence from both sides and make a decision, while appeals courts review the decisions made by trial courts. Sometimes rulings from appeals courts are appealed further to the U.S. Supreme Court or the state supreme courts.

Lawyers and courts refer to statutes and court decisions through a formal system of citations. Use of these citations reveals which court made the decision or which legislature passed the statute, and allows one to quickly locate the statute or court case online or in a law library. For example, the Supreme Court case *Brown v. Board of Education* has the legal citation 347 U.S. 483 (1954). At a law library, this 1954 decision can be found on page 483 of volume 347 of the U.S. Reports, which are the official collection of the Supreme Court's decisions. On the following page, you will find samples of all the major kinds of legal citation.

Finding sources of legal information on the Internet is relatively simple thanks to "portal" sites such as findlaw.com and lexisone.com, which allow the user to access a variety of constitutions, statutes, court opinions, law review articles, news articles, and other useful sources of information. For example, findlaw.com offers access to all Supreme Court decisions since 1893. Other useful sources of information include gpo.gov, which contains a complete copy of the U.S. Code, and thomas.loc.gov, which offers access to bills pending before Congress, as well as recently passed laws. Of course, the Internet changes every second of every day, so it is best to do some independent searching.

Of course, many people still do their research at law libraries, some of which are open to the public. For example, some state governments and universities offer the public access to their law collections. Law librarians can be of great assistance, as even experienced attorneys need help with legal research from time to time.

Common Citation Forms

Source of Law	Sample Citation	Notes
U.S. Supreme Court	*Employment Division v. Smith*, 485 U.S. 660 (1988)	The U.S. Reports is the official record of Supreme Court decisions. There is also an unofficial Supreme Court ("S. Ct.") reporter.
U.S. Court of Appeals	*United States v. Lambert*, 695 F.2d 536 (11th Cir.1983)	Appellate cases appear in the Federal Reporter, designated by "F." The 11th Circuit has jurisdiction in Alabama, Florida, and Georgia.
U.S. District Court	*Carillon Importers, Ltd. v. Frank Pesce Group, Inc.*, 913 F.Supp. 1559 (S.D.Fla.1996)	Federal trial-level decisions are reported in the Federal Supplement ("F. Supp."). Some states have multiple federal districts; this case originated in the Southern District of Florida.
U.S. Code	Thomas Jefferson Commemoration Commission Act, 36 U.S.C., §149 (2002)	Sometimes the popular names of legislation—names with which the public may be familiar—are included with the U.S. Code citation.
State Supreme Court	*Sterling v. Cupp*, 290 Ore. 611, 614, 625 P.2d 123, 126 (1981)	The Oregon Supreme Court decision is reported in both the state's reporter and the Pacific regional reporter.
State Statute	Pennsylvania Abortion Control Act of 1982, 18 Pa. Cons. Stat. 3203-3220 (1990)	States use many different citation formats for their statutes.

Cases

Winterbottom v. Wright (1842)

In this British case, the judge ruled that the victim of a product accident must have a contract with the seller in order to sue for damages. This law, which strongly limited the rights of plaintiffs to sue, prevailed in Britain and in the United States for several decades.

Brown v. Kendall, 60 Mass. (6 Cush) 292 (1850)

In this tort case, the court applied a negligence standard so that a plaintiff could aim to show the defendant did not meet a duty to exercise ordinary care.

Statler v. Ray Mfg. Co., 195 N.Y. 478, 480 (1909)

A court ruled in favor of a plaintiff, who was injured after a coffee urn exploded in a restaurant kitchen, because the manufacturer could reasonably foresee such harm and had a duty of care toward people who would use the machine.

MacPherson v. Buick Motor Co., 217 N.Y. 382, 111 N.E. 1050 (1916)

In this landmark case, the New York Court of Appeals ruled that individuals need not have a contract with the seller in order to recover damages for negligence. The court said the manufacturer owed a duty of care to the eventual consumers, not just to retail dealers.

Baxter v. Ford Motor Co., 168 Wash. 456, 12 P.2d 409 (1932)

A plaintiff who was injured during a car crash did not have a contract with the manufacturer (required at that time in product liability cases), since he bought his car from a dealer. He was still able to recover damages, however, under a theory of express warranty.

Escola v. Coca-Cola Bottling Co., 24 Cal.2d 453, 150 P.2d 436 (1944)

A restaurant employee was awarded damages for injuries that occurred after a glass soft-drink bottle exploded in her hand. The case is famous for its dissenting opinion, which advocated the doctrine of strict liability.

Henningsen v. Bloomfield Motors, Inc., 32 N.J. 358, 161 A.2d 69 (1960)

The plaintiff's new car malfunctioned and crashed while she was driving at a speed of 20 mph. The court said the manufacturer was liable because of an implied warranty that a product be fit and merchantable for its intended use(s).

Greenman v. Yuba Power Products, Inc., 59 Cal.2d 57, 27 Cal.Rptr. 697 (1963)

In this landmark case, a plaintiff who was severely injured after a machine malfunctioned sued the manufacturer and seller, alleging negligence and breach of warranty. The plaintiff won the case even though the court did not find negligence, and the California Supreme Court said that it was not necessary to find a breach of warranty.

Keener v. Dayton Electric Manufacturing Co., 445 S.W.2d 362, 364 (Mo. 1969)

The court used a theory of strict liability in finding for the plaintiff, whose husband died while handling a sump pump that was not equipped with a ground wire or overload protector. This product was therefore found to be defective under the law.

Grimshaw v. Ford Motor Co., **App. 174 Cal.Rptr. 348 (1981)**

In this first of the so-called "Pinto cases," the plaintiff died and her son was severely burned when their subcompact car exploded after being rear-ended (where the fuel tank was located). This case sparked new debates over risk/benefit analysis, since Ford had chosen *not* to implement design changes that would have made the car safer. The jury found for the plaintiffs and awarded punitive damages of $125 million (later reduced to $3.5 million).

Beshada v. Johns-Manville Prod. Corp., **447 A.2d 539 (N.J. 1982)**

In this case involving asbestos, the New Jersey court used a strict liability approach to reject the defense that the manufacturers' product and warnings were the state-of-the-art at that time.

Feldman v. Lederle Labs, **479 A.2d 374, (N.J. 1984)**

This case involved a "state-of-the-art" defense in regard to the defendant's medical product. The court held that manufacturers might have a duty to warn about dangers and risks that emerge after the initial approval and marketing processes take place.

Carrecter v. Colson Equipment Co., **499 A.2d 326, 330–31 (1985)**

In this Pennsylvania case, defendants were not allowed to use a defense that the design alternative was unavailable and scientifically knowable at the time they made their product. This evidence was excluded.

Browning-Ferris Industries v. Kelco Disposal, Inc., **492 U.S. 257 (1989)**

In this tort case, the federal appeals court ruled that the Excessive Fines Clause of the Eighth Amendment does not apply to punitive damages awards in cases between private parties.

Pacific Mutual Life Insurance Co. v. Haslip, **499 U.S. 1 (1991)**

The U.S. Supreme Court rejected the argument that punitive damages violate due process of law, as set forth in the U.S. Constitution.

Daubert v. Merrell Dow Pharmaceuticals, Inc., **509 U.S. 579, 589 (1993)**

The U.S. Supreme Court set standards for the kind of scientific testimony that can be heard in court, noting that judges must ensure that this kind of information has some foundation.

King v. Collagen Corporation, **983 F.2d 1130 (1st Cir. 1993);** *Stamps v. Collagen Corporation,* **984 F.2d 1416 (5th Cir. 1993)**

In these two cases, the courts ruled that the Medical Devices Amendment to the Food and Drug Act (1976) prevented the plaintiffs from suing the manufacturers of their medical implant materials.

Liebeck v. McDonald's Restaurants, P.T.S., Inc., **No. D-202 CV-93-02419, 1995 WL 360309 (Bernalillo County, N.M. Dist. Ct. Aug. 18, 1994)**

The plaintiff recovered compensatory and punitive damages after suffering severe burns from spilled coffee, purchased at a McDonald's drive-through. This case has become famous and controversial. Tort reform advocates have provided anecdotal versions of the case to promote their viewpoints.

BMW of North America, Inc. v. Gore, 517 U.S. 559 (1996)

The U.S. Supreme Court concluded that punitive damages could be deemed excessive. The Court did not set specific limits or ranges for these damages and has continued to refrain from setting dollar amounts.

Lakin v. Senco Products Inc., 144 Or App 52, 925 P.2d 107 (1996)

A plaintiff who suffered severe injuries after a nail gun misfired received less than $500,000 in noneconomic damages because of a law capping the amount of those damages. In 1999, a court later ruled that the $500,000 limit on noneconomic damages in personal injury and wrongful death actions arising out of common law violated the right to a jury trial provided by the Oregon State Constitution. Other states also have considered whether caps on damage awards are constitutional.

General Electric Co. v. Joiner, 522 U.S. 136 (1997)

This case affirmed the judge's role as a gatekeeper in applying the law in order to ensure that scientific evidence has enough merit to be heard in court. (See also *Daubert v. Merrell Dow Pharmaceuticals, Inc.*)

McMahon v. Bunn-O-Matic Corp., 150 F.3d 651 (7th circuit 1998)

In a case in which a plaintiff was burned by hot coffee, an Indiana court reasoned that this coffee was not defective because its temperature was within normal limits for coffee and that an adult consumer knows coffee is hot and can take precautions.

Axen v. American Home Products Corp., 158 Or. App. 292, 974 P.2d 224 (1999)

An Oregon Court of Appeals held that a punitive damages award was not excessive. The lower court concluded that the pharmaceutical company that sold the medication taken by the plaintiff knew it could cause blindness but failed to adequately warn people about this serious side effect.

Philip Morris USA v. Williams, 549 U.S. 346 (2007)

The estate of a heavy smoker who died of lung cancer sued the cigarette maker and was awarded $821,000 in compensatory damages and $79.5 million in punitive damages. The defendant appealed on the basis that the jury had awarded these high punitive damages by considering the damage done to other smokers who were not part of the lawsuit. The U.S. Supreme Court held that juries cannot base punitive damages awards on their desire to punish the defendant for harm caused to people other than the plaintiff who is before the court.

Riegel v. Medtronic, Inc., 552 U.S. (2008)

The U.S. Supreme Court upheld a federal act that says lawsuits against medical devices cannot go forward in any state if the device has undergone FDA premarket approval.

Statutes

Interstate Commerce Act of 1887

This act led to the formation of the Interstate Commerce Commission, which is regarded as the first true federal regulatory agency. The agency initially aimed to prevent railroad abuse and discrimination so that farmers and small businesses could transport goods, but it has expanded its activities through the years.

Medical Devices Amendment to the Food and Drug Act (1976)

This act specifies the duties of the FDA in approving and regulating medical devices. Courts have applied it to cases where people filed lawsuits involving medical devices that received FDA approval.

National Childhood Vaccine Injury Act (1986)

This federal program was set up to compensate victims of vaccine-related injuries or deaths while protecting manufacturers from product liability lawsuits so they would continue to develop and sell vaccines.

General Aviation Revitalization Act of 1994

This act aimed to revive the domestic private aircraft industry by setting specific time limits on product liability lawsuits involving these aircraft and their components, including an 18-year statute of repose.

Biomaterials Access Assurance Act of 1998

This federal act protects the suppliers of bulk components and raw materials for implants from lawsuits, regardless of state laws, and applies to all such materials "except the silicone gel and the silicone envelope utilized in a breast implant containing silicone gel."

Class Action Fairness Act of 2005

This act expanded federal jurisdiction over many class-action lawsuits in order to reduce "forum shopping" in the state courts, as well as expanded federal scrutiny over these cases. The act set rules for settlements, especially those involving coupons, rather than money, for plaintiffs, as well as cases in which attorney fees exceeded the amount of the settlement so that victims are required to pay instead of receiving any compensation themselves.

Consumer Product Safety Improvement Act of 2008

The Consumer Product Safety Commission (CPSC) establishes mandatory testing on all children's products, bans lead in children's toys, and aims to inform the public more quickly when potential problems emerge.

Terms and Concepts

Assumption of risk
Breach of warranty
Caveat emptor
Class-action lawsuit
Collateral source rule
Common law
Comparative negligence
Compensatory damages
Contingent fees

Terms and Concepts *(continued)*

Contributory negligence
Damages
Defect
Duty
Economic damages
Failure to warn
Federalism
Forum shopping
Joint and several liability
Jurisdiction
Liability
Manufacturing defect
Mass tort
Misuse of product
Negligence
Noneconomic damages
Punitive damages
Remittitur
State-of-the-art defense
Statute
Statute of limitations
Statute of repose
Strict liability
Tort
Warranty (express)
Warranty (implied)

NOTES

Introduction: Product Liability in America

1 *Liebeck v. McDonald's Restaurants, P.T.S., Inc.*, No. D-202 CV-93-02419, 1995 WL 360309 (Bernalillo County, N.M. Dist. Ct., Aug. 18, 1994).

2 *McMahon v. Bunn-O-Matic Corp.*, 150 F.3d 651 (7th circuit 1998).

3 Lawrence J. McQuillan and Hovannes Abramyan, "The Tort Tax," *Wall Street Journal*, March 27, 2007, http://online. wsj.com/article/SB117496524456750056. html.

4 Philip K. Howard, *The Collapse of the Common Good: How America's Lawsuit Culture Undermines Our Freedom.* New York: Ballantine Books, 2002, p. 29.

5 Walton H. Hamilton, "The Ancient Maxim Caveat Emptor," 40 *Yale Law Journal*, 1931, p. 1164.

6 Hamilton, p. 1150.

7 152 ER 402 from Exchequer-Chamber, in Martin Philip Golding, *Legal Reasoning.* Peterborough, Ontario: Broadview Press, 2001, p. 113.

8 Lawrence M. Friedman, *A History of American Law.* New York: Simon and Schuster, 1973, pp. 409–410.

9 *Brown v. Kendall*, 60 Mass. (6 Cush) 292 (1850).

10 *Haring v. New York and Erie Railroad*, 13 Barb.2 (New York 1852).

11 *Devlin v. Smith*, 89 N.Y. 470 (1882).

12 *Statler v. Ray Mfg. Co.*, 195 N.Y. 478, 480 (1909).

13 *MacPherson v. Buick Motor Co.*, 217 N.Y. 382, 111 N.E. 1050 (1916). Donald C. MacPherson, Buick Motor Co. Court of Appeals, N.Y., http://www.courts.state. ny.us/reporter/archives/ macpherson_buick.htm.

14 Ibid.

15 *Adams v. Bullock*, 227 N.Y. 208, 125 N.E. 93, Court of Appeals of N.Y. (1919).

16 *Baxter v. Ford Motor Co.*, 168 Wash. 456, 12 P.2d 409 (1932).

17 *Escola v. Coca-Cola Bottling Co.*, 24 Cal.2d 453, 150 P.2d 436 (1944).

18 *Greenman v. Yuba Power Products, Inc.*, 59 Cal.2d 57, 27 Cal.Rptr. 697 (1963).

19 *Larsen v. General Motors Corp.*, 391 F.2d 495 (8th Cir. 1968).

20 *Keener v. Dayton Electric Manufacturing Co.*, 445 S.W.2d 362, 364 (Mo. 1969).

21 *Beshada v. Johns-Manville Prod. Corp.*, 447 A.2d 539 (N.J. 1982).

22 *Feldman v. Lederle Labs*, 479 A.2d 374 (N.J. 1984).

23 *Liability Insurance Availability.* U.S. Congress: House Committee on Energy and Commerce. Hearings before the Subcommittee on Commerce, Transportation, and Tourism of the Committee on Energy and Commerce. House of Representatives, Ninety-Ninth Congress. Part 3. U.S. Government Printing Office, 1987, p. 310.

24 W. Kip Viscusi, "Liability," The Concise Encyclopedia of Economics, http://www. econlib.org/library/Enc1/Liability.html.

25 W. Kip Viscusi, *Reforming Products Liability.* Cambridge, Mass.: Harvard University Press, 1991, pp. 3–4.

26 Robert W. Sturgis, *Tort Cost Trends: An International Perspective.* Simsbury, Conn.: Tillinghast, 1989, p. 16.

27 ATRA. "Product Liability Reform," http://www.atra.org/show/7341.

28 David G. Owen and Jerry J. Phillips, *Products Liability in a Nutshell.* Eagen, Minn.: Thomson/West, 2005, p. 234.

Point: Federal Liability Laws Are Needed

1 Oliver Wendell Holmes, Jr., *The Path of the Law.* Whitefish, Mont.: Kessinger Publishing, 2004, p. 6.

2 Oliver Wendell Holmes, Jr., "The Path of the Law," 10 *Harvard Law Review* 457, 1897, http://www.constitution.org/lrev/ owh/path_law.htm.

3 Owen and Phillips, p. 233.

4 Introduction: S-648 Product Liability Reform Act of 1997, http://thomas.loc. gov/cgi-bin/cpquery/T?&report=sr032& dbname=105&.

5 Richard L. Lippke, *Radical Business Ethics.* Lanham, Md.: Rowman & Littlefield Publishers, Inc., 1995, p. 168.

6 *Carrecter v. Colson Equipment Co.*, 499 A.2d 326, 330–31 (1985).

7 Howard, *The Collapse of the Common Good*, p. 21.

8 *Travis v. Harris Corp.*, 565 F.2d 443, 447 (7th Cir. 1977).

129

9 Francis P. Manchisi and Lorraine E.J. Gallagher, "A Nationwide Survey of Statutes of Repose." March 2006, http://www.wilsonelser.com/files/repository/NatlSurveyRepose_March2006.pdf.

10 Oregon Law Commission, "A Report to the Statutes of Limitations Work Group Regarding Statutory Time Limitations on Product Liability Actions." July 2000, http://www.willamette.edu/wucl/pdf/olc/statutes_limitations_report.pdf.

11 Clark Embler, "Pollution and Liability," *The Corporate Board*, May/June 1987, p. 13.

12 Michael Ena, "Choice of Law and Predictability of Decisions in Products Liability Cases," *Fordham Urban Law Journal*, November 28, 2007, p. 1418.

13 *Lakin v. Senco Products Inc.*, 144 Or App 52, 925 P.2d 107 (1996).

14 *Williams v. Philip Morris, Inc.*, 182 Or App 44, 48 P.3d 824 (2002).

15 Stephen B. Presser, "How Should the Law of Products Liability be Harmonized? What Americans Can Learn from Europeans," Manhattan Institute for Policy Research, Global Liability Issues, Vol. 2, February 2002, http://www.manhattan-institute.org/html/gli_2.htm.

16 Richard Neely, *The Product Liability Mess: How Business Can Be Rescued from the Politics of State Courts*, New York: Simon and Schuster, 1988.

17 *Riegel v. Medtronic, Inc.*, 552 U.S. (2008).

18 Viscusi, *Reforming Products Liability*, p. 155.

19 Ibid., pp. 155–156.

20 Ibid., p. 156.

21 S. 648 Product Liability Reform Act of 1997 (Introduced in Senate), http://thomas.loc.gov/cgi-bin/query/z?c105:S.5:'.

22 Calvin A. Campbell, Jr., President and CEO Goodman Equipment Corporation, quoted in *Product Liability Standards: Hearings Before the Subcommittee on Commerce, Consumer Protection, and Competitiveness of the Committee on Energy and Commerce.* House of Representatives, One Hundred Third Congress, Second Session, on H.R. 1910, A Bill to Establish Uniform Product Liability Standards, February 2, April 21, and May 3, 1994. Washington, D.C.: U.S. Government Printing Office, 1994, p. 93.

23 Luigi Mastroianni, Peter J. Donaldson, and Thomas T. Kane, eds. *Developing New Contraceptives: Obstacles and Opportunities.* National Academies Press, 1990, p. 141.

24 Presser, "How Should the Law . . ."

25 Ibid.

26 *Product Liability Standards*, p. 104.

27 E. Patrick McGuire, *The Impact of Product Liability.* New York: The Conference Board, Inc., 1988, p. 1.

Counterpoint: Federal Liability Laws Are Unnecessary

1 *United States v. Lopez*, 514 U.S. 549, 577 (1995).

2 Ibid.

3 Ibid.

4 *State Farm Mutual Auto Ins. Co. v. Campbell*, 538 U.S. 408 (2003).

5 U.S. Department of Justice Report, Civil Justice Statistics for 1996, http://www.ojp.usdoj.gov/bjs/civil.htm.

6 *Kelso v. Union Pacific Railroad Co.*, et. al., 179 Ill.2d 367 (1997).

7 Robert S. Peck, "Defending the American System of Justice." *Trial* 18, April 2001.

8 Quoted in Jacqueline Calmes, "Congress to Face Product Liability Bill in 1985," *Congressional Quarterly Weekly Online*, December 8, 1984, pp. 3067–3071.

9 Emily Umbright, "Report Finds Products Liability Cases on the Decline," *Daily Record* (St. Louis, Mo./St. Louis Countian), July 10, 2006.

10 *King v. Collagen Corporation*, 983 F.2d 1130 (1st Cir. 1993); *Stamps v. Collagen Corporation*, 984 F.2d 1416 (5th Cir. 1993).

11 *Product Liability Standards*, p. 142.

12 *Hillsborough County v. Automated Medical Laboratories, Inc.*, 471 U.S. 707 (1985).

13 *Metropolitan Life Ins. Co. v. Massachusetts*, 471 U.S. 724 (1985).

14 Alexei Barrionuevo, "As U.S. Imports More Food, FDA Falters," *New York Times*, May 1, 2007, http://www.nytimes.com/2007/05/01/business/

worldbusiness/01iht-fda.1.5513381.
html.

**Point: Strict Liability Standards
Cause Economic Problems**

1 *Goodyear Tire & Rubber Co, v. Kirby*,
   (Miss. App. Ct. 2009).

2 *MacPherson v. Buick Motor Co.*, 217 N.Y.
   382, 111 N.E. 1050 (1916).

3 Catherine Crier, *The Case Against Law-
   yers: How the Lawyers, Politicians, and
   Bureaucrats Have Turned the Law Into
   an Instrument of Tyranny and What We
   As Citizens Have to Do About It*. New
   York: Random House, 2003, p. 81.

4 Lynn Langton and Thomas H. Cohen,
   "Civil Bench and Jury Trials in State
   Courts, 2005." U.S. Department of Justice, Bureau of Justice Statistics, 2008,
   http://www.ojp.usdoj.gov/bjs/pub/pdf/
   cbjtsc05.pdf.

5 National Small Business Association, "Product Liability Reform: Issue
   Brief," http://www.nsba.biz/docs/
   product_liability_reform.pdf.

6 American Tort Reform Association
   (ATRA). "Product Liability Reform,"
   http://www.atra.org/issues/index.
   php?issue=7341.

7 Quoted in McGuire, p. 11.

8 Lawrence J. McQuillan, et. al. "Jackpot
   Justice: The True Cost of America's
   Tort System," Pacific Research Insti-
   tute, March 2007, p. 32, http://www.
   legalreforminthenews.com/2007PDFS/
   PRI_2007JackpotJusticeFinal.pdf.

9 American Tort Reform Association
   (ATRA). "Punitive Damages Reform,"
   http://www.atra.org/show/7343.

10 McQuillan, et. al., pp. 34–35.

11 Bob Dorigo Jones, "Wacky Warning
    Labels Reflect High Cost of Liability
    Rulings," *Detroit News*, May 12, 2009.

12 National Small Business Association,
    "Product Liability Reform: Issue Brief."

13 Property Casualty Insurers Association
    of America, "Tort Tax Hurts Americans
    Even More Than Previously Thought,"
    PCI News, March 27, 2007, http://www.
    pciaa.net/publish/web/webpress.nsf/
    eaab008f9ddd474f862569df0065e618/
    86256bf40081c83b862572ab005435dc/
    $FILE/PCI%20TortTax-PRI%20Study.

pdf; Also: McQuillan, et. al. "Jackpot
Justice," p. 35.

14 *Product Liability Standards*, p. 93.

15 Quoted in Property Casualty Insurers
    Association of America, "Tort Tax Hurts
    Americans Even More Than Previously
    Thought."

16 *Product Liability Standards*, p. 63.

17 Ibid.

18 Ibid.

19 Viscusi, *Reforming Products Liability*, p. 8.

20 W. Kip Viscusi, "Liability."

21 Henry Grabowski, "Product Liability in
    Pharmaceuticals: Comments on Chap-
    ters Eight and Nine," in Peter W. Huber
    and Robert E. Litan, eds., *The Liability
    Maze: The Impact of Liability Law on
    Safety and Innovation*. Washington,
    D.C.: The Brookings Institution, 1991,
    p. 360.

22 Ibid.

23 Steven Greenhouse, "Searle Backs
    Medical Device," *New York Times*,
    October 9, 1985, http://www.nytimes.
    com/1985/10/09/business/
    searle-backs-medical-device.html.

24 Luigi Mastroianni, Jr., Peter J. Donald-
    son, and Thomas T. Kane, eds., *Develop-
    ing New Contraceptives: Obstacles and
    Opportunities*. National Academies
    Press, 1990, p. 141.

25 Crier, p. 75.

26 *Product Liability Reform Act of 1997:
    Report of the Committee on Commerce,
    Science, and Transportation on S. 648
    Together with Minority Views*, http://
    thomas.loc.gov/cgi-bin/cpquery/
    T?&report=sr032&dbname=105&.

27 George L. Priest, "Products Liability Law
    and the Accident Rate," in Robert E.
    Litan and Clifford Winston, eds., *Liabil-
    ity: Perspectives and Policy*. Washington,
    D.C.: The Brookings Institution, 1988,
    pp. 187–194.

28 John D. Graham, "Product Liability and
    Motor Vehicle Safety," in Huber and
    Litan, p. 183.

29 Ibid.

30 Graham, p. 184.

31 National Safety Center Report, 1988,
    p. 10, cited in Viscusi, *Reforming Prod-
    ucts Liability*, p. 19.

131

32 W. Kip Viscusi, "Liability," *The Concise Encyclopedia of Economics*. 2nd ed., http://www.econlib.org/library/Enc/Liability.html.

33 John Hasnas, "The Mirage of Product Safety," in George G. Brenkert and Tom L. Beauchamp, eds., *The Oxford Handbook of Business Ethics*. Oxford, England: Oxford University Press, 2009.

34 *McMahon v. Bunn-O-Matic Corp.* 150 F.3d 651 (7th circuit 1998).

35 Debra Rae Anderson, "The Cost of Frivolous Lawsuits Is No Joke," *Minneapolis/St. Paul Business Journal*, August 8, 1997, http://www.bizjournals.com/twincities/stories/1997/08/11/editorial2.html.

36 *Kroger Co. Sav-On Store v. Presnell*, 515 N.E.2d 538, 543 (Ind. Ct. App. 1987).

37 Ibid.

38 *Todd v. Societe BIC*, S.A. 9 F.3d 1216, 1218–19 (7th Cir. 1993).

39 Jane Stapleton, *Product Liability*. Cambridge, England: Cambridge University Press, 1994, p. 33.

Counterpoint: Strict Liability Standards Protect People

1 *Irion v. Sun Lighting, Inc.*, 2004 WL 746823 (Tenn. Ct. App. 4/7/2004).

2 Ralph Nader, *The Ralph Nader Reader*. New York: Seven Stories Press, 2000, p. 281.

3 Langton and Cohen, "Civil Bench and Jury Trials in State Courts, 2005."

4 National Center for State Courts (NCSC), "Court Statistics Project," 2007, http://www.ncsconline.org/D_Research/csp/CSP_Main_Page.html.

5 Ibid.

6 Robert S. Peck, "A Time for Facts, Not Overblown Anecdotes," RAND Review, Summer 2004, http://www.rand.org/publications/randreview/issues/summer2004/44.html.

7 Michael G. Shanley and Mark A. Peterson, "Posttrial Adjustments to Jury Awards," RAND ICJ Report, 1987, http://www.rand.org/pubs/reports/R3511/.

8 Towers Perrin/Tillinghast. U.S. Tort Costs: 2004 Summary: Trends and Findings of the Cost of the U.S. Tort System, p. 2, http://www.towersperrin.com/tillinghast/publications/reports/Tort_2004/Tort.pdf.

9 Tillinghast–Towers Perrin. *U.S. Tort Costs: 2004 Update: Trends and Findings on the Cost of the U.S. Tort System*, 2004, https://www.towersperrin.com/tillinghast/publications/reports/Tort_2004/Tort.pdf.

10 Risk and Insurance Management Society (RIMS), *1994 Cost of Risk Survey*.

11 "Product Liability Is not a Major Factor in the Competitiveness of U.S. Business." In Senate Report 105-032: Product Liability Reform Act of 1997, http://thomas.loc.gov/cgi-bin/cpquery/?&sid=cp1053xOTt&refer=&r_n=sr032.105&db_id=105&item=&sel=TOC_295538&RIMS.

12 Nader, pp. 276, 275–278.

13 *Product Liability Standards*, p. 272.

14 Quoted in *Product Liability Standards*, p. 271.

15 Nicholas A. Ashford and Robert F. Stone, "Liability, Innovation, and Safety in the Chemical Industry," in Huber and Litan, eds., *The Liability Maze*, pp. 367–427.

16 Nathan Weber, *Product Liability: The Corporate Response*. New York: The Conference Board, 1987, p. 2.

17 W. Kip Viscusi and Michael J. Moore, "An Industrial Profile of the Links between Product Liability and Innovation," in Huber and Litan, eds., p. 114.

18 Nader, p. 32.

19 Testimony of Professor Mark Hager, Assistant Professor of Law, Washington College of Law, American University, at Consumer Subcommittee Hearing on S. 1400, April 5, 1990, http://thomas.loc.gov/cgi-bin/cpquery/31?&sid=cp105BUdra&l_f=1&l_file=list/cp105cs.lst&hd_count=50&l_t=417&refer=&r_n=sr032.105&db_id=105&item=31&sel=TOC_272541&.

20 George G. Brenkert, "Strict Products Liability and Compensatory Justice," in Tom L. Beauchamp, et. al., eds., *Ethical Theory and Business*. Upper Saddle River, N.J.: Prentice Hall, 2008, pp. 189 ff.

21 *Escola v. Coca-Cola Bottling Co.*, 24 Cal.2d 453, 150 P.2d 436 (1944).
22 Owen and Phillips, p. 142.
23 Ibid.
24 *Greenman v. Yuba Power Products, Inc.*, 59 Cal.2d 57 (1963).

Point: Courts Should Have Less Discretion in Awarding Damages

1 *BMW of North America, Inc. v. Gore*, 517 U.S. 559 (1996).
2 Linda Greenhouse, "For First Time, Justices Reject Punitive Award," *New York Times*, May 21, 1996.
3 *BMW of North America, Inc. v. Gore*, 517 U.S. 559 (1996).
4 Ibid.
5 American Tort Reform Association, "Punitive Damages Reform," http://www.atra.org/show/7343.
6 *State Farm Mutual Auto Ins. v. Campbell*, 538 U.S. 408 (2003).
7 *BMW of North America, Inc. v. Gore*, 517 U.S. 559 (1996).
8 Ibid.
9 American Tort Reform Association, "Punitive Damages Reform."
10 Product Liability Reform Bill of 1997.
11 Product Liability Reform Bill of 1997, Section 5.
12 Doug Bandow, "Exploding Jury Awards Bode Ill for U.S. Economy in 21st Century," The Cato Institute, March 6, 2000, http://www.cato.org/pub_display.php?pub_id=4768.
13 Quoted in Peter Schuler, "Inconsistencies Evident between the Monetary, Moral Judgments of Juries," *The University of Chicago Chronicle*, March 28, 2002, http://chronicle.uchicago.edu/020328/sunstein.shtml.
14 *BMW of North America, Inc. v. Gore*, 517 U.S. 559 (1996).
15 American Tort Reform Association, "Punitive Damages Reform."
16 Cass R. Sunstein, *Punitive Damages: How Juries Decide.* Chicago: University of Chicago Press, 2002, pp. 242, 252–253.
17 Sunstein, p. 26.
18 Quoted in Schuler, "Inconsistencies Evident between the Monetary, Moral Judgments of Juries."
19 Sunstein, p. 75.
20 Quoted in Schuler, "Inconsistencies Evident between the Monetary, Moral Judgments of Juries."
21 Paul H. Rubin, "Tort Reform Saves Lives," *Wall Street Journal*, October 8, 2005, http://online.wsj.com/article/SB112873085838663424.html.
22 Ibid.

Counterpoint: Courts Should Have Discretion in Awarding Damages

1 Quoted in Alicia Mundy, *Dispensing With the Truth: The Victims, the Drug Companies, and the Dramatic Story Behind the Battle Over Fen-phen*, New York: St. Martin's Press, 2002, p. 220.
2 *Axen v. American Home Products Corp.*, 158 Or. App. 292, 974 P.2d 224 (1999).
3 Michael Rustad and Thomas H. Koenig, *Demystifying Punitive Damages in Product Liability Cases: A Survey of a Quarter Century of Trial Verdicts.* Roscoe Pound Foundation, 1991; Michael Rustad, "In Defense of Punitive Damages in Products Liability: Testing Tort Anecdotes with Empirical Data," 78 *Iowa Law Review* 1 (1992).
4 RAND, "Punitive Damages in Financial Injury Verdicts," http://www.rand.org/pubs/monograph_reports/MR889/MR889.text.html.
5 U.S. Department of Justice, Bureau of Justice Statistics, August 2000.
6 Erik Moller, Nicholas M. Pace, and Stephen J. Carroll, *Punitive Damages in Financial Injury Jury Verdicts.* RAND Institute for Civil Justice, 1997.
7 Langton and Cohen, "Civil Bench and Jury Trials in State Courts, 2005."
8 Margaret Cronin Fisk, "Billion-Dollar U.S. Verdicts Vanish After Appeals, New Rulings," Bloomberg News, January 8, 2009, http://www.bloomberg.com/apps/news?pid=20601127&sid=a3pNSz7zXQTk&refer=law.
9 Owen and Phillips, p. 493.
10 *Barnett v. la Societe Anonyme Turbomeca France,* (Mo. Ct. App. 1997).
11 David Margolick, "G.M. Verdict Intensifies Debate on Jury Awards," *New York Times*, February 6, 1993, http://www.

133

nytimes.com/1993/02/06/us/gm-verdict-intensifies-debate-on-jury-awards.html.

12 Viscusi, *Reforming Products Liability*, p. 2.

13 Ibid.

14 *Grimshaw v. Ford Motor Co.*, App. 174 Cal. Rptr. 348 (1981).

15 *Gilham v. Admiral Corp.*, 6th Cir. 1975.

16 *Product Liability Standards*, p. 67.

17 Morton Mintz, "A Crime Against Women: A.H. Robins and the Dalkon Shield," *The Multinational Monitor*, January 15, 1986, http://multinationalmonitor.org/hyper/issues/1986/0115/index.html.

18 Neil Vidmar and Valerie P. Hans, *American Juries: The Verdict*. Amherst, N.Y.: Prometheus, 2007, p. 314. Linda K. Enghagen and Anthony Gilardi, "McDonald's and the $2.9-million Cup of Coffee: Putting Things in Perspective," *Cornell Hospitality Quarterly*, June 1, 2002.

19 Langton and Cohen, "Civil Bench and Jury Trials in State Courts, 2005."

20 Theodore Eisenberg, et. al., "Juries, Judges, and Punitive Damages: An Empirical Study," *Cornell Law Review*, Vol. 87:743, 2001–2002, pp. 744–782, http://library2.lawschool.cornell.edu/hein/Eisenberg%20Theodore%2087%20Cornell%20L.%20Rev.%20743%20(2002).pdf. William Glaberson, "A Study's Verdict: Jury Awards Are Not Out of Control," *New York Times*, August 6, 2001, http://www.nytimes.com/2001/08/06/us/a-study-s-verdict-jury-awards-are-not-out-of-control.html.

21 *Silkwood v. Kerr McGee Corp.*, 464 U.S. 238, 255 (1984).

22 *Wilkes v. Wood*, 98 Eng. Rep. 489 (C.P. 1763).

23 *Day v. Woodworth*, 54 U.S. 13 How. 363, 371 (1851).

24 Ibid.

25 Ibid.

26 *Browning-Ferris Industries v. Kelco Disposal, Inc.*, 492 U.S. 257 (1989).

27 *Axen v. American Home Products Corp.*, 158 Or. App. 292, 974 P.2d 224 (1999).

28 *Pacific Mutual Life Insurance Co. v. Haslip*, 499 U.S. 1 (1991).

29 *TXO Production Corp. v. Alliance Resources*, 509 U.S. 443 (1993).

30 *BMW of North America, Inc. v. Gore*, 517 U.S. 559 (1996).

31 *State Farm Mutual Auto Ins. Co. v. Campbell*, 538 U.S. 408 (2003).

32 Fisk, "Billion-Dollar U.S. Verdicts Vanish After Appeals, New Rulings."

Conclusion: Debates Go On

1 Congressional Record, Proceedings and Debates of the 108th Congress, Second Session, Vol. 150, No. 92, July 7, 2004, http://feinstein.senate.gov/04Speeches/class-action07.htm.

2 Ibid.

3 Ibid.

4 Quoted in John F. Harris and William Branigin, "Bush Signs Class-Action Changes Into Law," *Washington Post*, February 18, 2005, http://www.washingtonpost.com/wp-dyn/articles/A35084-2005Feb18.html.

5 Viscusi, *Reforming Products Liability*, p. 158.

6 Crier, p. 185.

7 Walter K. Olson, *The Rule of Lawyers: How the New Litigation Elite Threatens America's Rule of Law*. New York: Macmillan, 2004, p. 19.

8 D. Alan Rudlin, ed., *Toxic Tort Litigation*. Chicago: American Bar Association, 2007, p. 362.

9 Ibid.

10 Crier, p. 13.

11 "Crown Cork and Seal Wins Asbestos Case," FoodProductionDaily.com, June 13, 2002, http://www.foodproductiondaily.com/Supply-Chain/Crown-Cork-and-Seal-wins-asbestos-case.

12 Ken Dilanian, "Amendment Limits Asbestos Liability in Mergers," *Central Penn Business Journal*, December 7, 2001, http://www.allbusiness.com/north-america/united-states-pennsylvania/991612-1.html.

13 Michael Simento, *Silicone Breast Implants: Why Has Science Been Ignored?* American Council on Science and Health, Inc., 1996, http://www.fumento.com/breastbook.pdf. Karen Springen

and Mary Hager, "Silicone: Juries Vs. Science," *Newsweek*, November 13, 1995, http://www.newsweek.com/id/104075.

14 *Daubert v. Merrell Dow Pharmaceuticals, Inc.*, 509 U.S. 579, 589 (1993).

15 *General Electric Co. v. Joiner*, 522 U.S. 136 (1997).

16 McGuire, p. 25.

17 "National Rifle Association Ranked No. 1 on FORTUNE Power 25 List," Business Wire, May 14, 2001, http://www.allbusiness.com/government/elections-politics-politics-political-parties/6122748-1.html. Jeffrey H. Birnbaum, "Washington's Power 25," *Fortune*, December 8, 1997, http://money.cnn.com/magazines/fortune/fortune_archive/1997/12/08/234927/index.htm. Jeffrey H. Birnbaum and Natasha Graves, "Follow the Money Hard Money," *Fortune*, December 6, 1999, http://money.cnn.com/magazines/fortune/fortune_archive/1999/12/06/269954/index.htm.

18 Olson, p. 300.

19 John Cochran, "'Tort Reform' Battle: A Simple Case of Complexity," *Congressional Quarterly Weekly*, January 29, 2005.

20 Huber and Litan, p. vii.

21 Cochran, "'Tort Reform' Battle: A Simple Case of Complexity."

RESOURCES ||||▷

Books

Beauchamp, Tom L., et. al., eds. *Ethical Theory and Business*. Upper Saddle River, N.J.: Prentice Hall, 2008.

Brenkert, George G., and Tom L. Beauchamp, eds. *The Oxford Handbook of Business Ethics*. Oxford, England: Oxford University Press, 2009.

Buckley, William R., and Cathy J. Okrent. *Torts & Personal Injury Law*. Florence, Ky.: Cengage Learning, 2003.

Crier, Catherine. *The Case Against Lawyers: How the Lawyers, Politicians, and Bureaucrats Have Turned the Law Into an Instrument of Tyranny and What We As Citizens Have to Do About It*. New York: Random House, 2003.

Friedman, Lawrence M. *A History of American Law*. New York: Simon and Schuster, 1973.

Golden, Martin Philip. *Legal Reasoning*. Peterborough, Ontario: Broadview Press, 2001.

Goodden, Randall L. *Product Liability Prevention: A Strategic Guide*. Milwaukee, Wis.: ASQ Quality Press, 2000.

Haltom, William, and Michael McCann. *Distorting the Law: Politics, Media, and the Litigation Crisis*. Chicago: University of Chicago Press, 2004.

Holmes, Oliver Wendell, Jr. *The Path of the Law*. Whitefish, Mont.: Kessinger Publishing, 2004.

Howard, Philip K. *The Collapse of the Common Good: How America's Lawsuit Culture Undermines Our Freedom*. New York: Ballantine Books, 2002.

———. *Life Without Lawyers: Liberating Americans From Too Much Law*. New York: W.W. Norton & Co., 2009.

Huber, Peter W., and Robert E. Litan, eds. *The Liability Maze: The Impact of Liability Law on Safety and Innovation*. Washington, D.C.: The Brookings Institution, 1991.

Litan, Robert E., and Clifford Winston, eds. *Liability: Perspectives and Policy*. Washington, D.C.: The Brookings Institution, 1988.

Mastroianni, Luigi, Peter J. Donaldson, and Thomas T. Kane. *Developing New Contraceptives: Obstacles and Opportunities.* National Academies Press, 1990.

McGuire, E. Patrick. *The Impact of Product Liability.* New York: The Conference Board, Inc., 1988.

Moller, Erik, Nicholas M. Pace, and Stephen J. Carroll. *Punitive Damages in Financial Injury Jury Verdicts.* Rand Institute for Civil Justice, 1997.

Mundy, Alicia. *Dispensing With the Truth: The Victims, the Drug Companies, and the Dramatic Story Behind the Battle Over Fen-phen.* New York: St. Martin's Press, 2002.

Nader, Ralph. *The Ralph Nader Reader.* New York: Seven Stories Press, 2000.

Neely, Richard. *The Product Liability Mess: How Business Can Be Rescued from the Politics of State Courts.* New York: Simon and Schuster, 1988.

Olson, Walter K. *The Rule of Lawyers: How the New Litigation Elite Threatens America's Rule of Law.* New York: Macmillan, 2004.

O'Malley, Pat. *Risk, Uncertainty and Government.* New York: Cavendish, 2004.

Owen, David G., and Jerry J. Phillips. *Products Liability in a Nutshell.* Eagen, Minn.: Thomson/West, 2005.

Product Liability Standards: Hearings Before the Subcommittee on Commerce, Consumer Protection, and Competitiveness of the Committee on Energy and Commerce. House of Representatives, One Hundred Third Congress, Second Session, on H.R. 1910, A Bill to Establish Uniform Product Liability Standards, February 2, April 21, and May 3, 1994. Washington D.C.: U.S. Government Printing Office, 1994.

Rudlin, D. Alan, ed. *Toxic Tort Litigation.* Chicago: American Bar Association, 2007.

Rustad, Michael, and Thomas H. Koenig. *Demystifying Punitive Damages in Product Liability Cases: A Survey of a Quarter Century of Trial Verdicts.* Roscoe Pound Foundation, 1991.

Simento, Michael. *Silicone Breast Implants: Why Has Science Been Ignored?* New York: American Council on Science and Health, Inc., 1996.

Stapleton, Jane. *Product Liability*. Cambridge, England: Cambridge University Press, 1994.

Sturgis, Robert W. *Tort Cost Trends: An International Perspective*. Simsbury, Conn.: Tillinghast, 1989.

Sunstein, Cass R., et al. *Punitive Damages: How Juries Decide*. Chicago: University of Chicago Press, 2002.

Vidmar, Neil, and Valerie P. Hans. *American Juries: The Verdict*. Amherst: Prometheus, 2007.

Viscusi, W. Kip. *Reforming Products Liability*. Cambridge, Mass.: Harvard University Press, 1991.

Weber, Nathan. *Product Liability: The Corporate Response*. New York: The Conference Board, 1987.

Articles

Anderson, Debra Rae. "The Cost of Frivolous Lawsuits Is No Joke," *Minneapolis/St. Paul Business Journal*, August 8, 1997. Available online. URL: http://www.bizjournals.com/twincities/stories/1997/08/11/editorial2.html.

Bandow, Doug. "Exploding Jury Awards Bode Ill for U.S. Economy in 21st Century," The Cato Institute, March 6, 2000. Available online. URL: http://www.cato.org/pub_display.php?pub_id=4768.

Birnbaum, Jeffrey H. "Washington's Power 25," *Fortune*, December 8, 1997. Available online. URL: http://money.cnn.com/magazines/fortune/fortune_archive/1997/12/08/234927/index.htm.

Birnbaum, Jeffrey H., and Natasha Graves. "Follow the Money Hard Money," *Fortune*, December 6, 1999. Available online. URL: http://money.cnn.com/magazines/fortune/fortune_archive/1999/12/06/269954/index.htm.

Calmes, Jacqueline. "Congress to Face Product Liability Bill in 1985," *Congressional Quarterly Weekly*, December 8, 1984, pp. 3067–3071.

Cochran, John. "'Tort Reform' Battle: A Simple Case of Complexity," *Congressional Quarterly Weekly*, January 29, 2005.

"Crown Cork and Seal Wins Asbestos Case." FoodProductionDaily.com, June 13, 2002. Available online. URL: http://www.foodproductiondaily. com/Supply-Chain/Crown-Cork-and-Seal-wins-asbestos-case.

Eisenberg, Theodore, et. al. "Juries, Judges, and Punitive Damages: An Empirical Study," *Cornell Law Review*, Vol. 87:743, 2001–2002, pp. 744–782. Available online. URL: http://library2.lawschool.cornell.edu/hein/ Eisenberg%20Theodore%2087%20Cornell%20L.%20Rev.%20743%20(2 002).pdf.

Embler, Clark. "Pollution and Liability," *The Corporate Board*, May/June 1987.

Ena, Michael. "Choice of Law and Predictability of Decisions in Products Liability Cases," *Fordham Urban Law Journal*, November 28, 2007, pp. 1417–1456.

Enghagen, Linda K., and Anthony Gilardi. "McDonald's and the $2.9-million Cup of Coffee: Putting Things in Perspective," *Cornell Hospitality Quarterly*, June 1, 2002.

Fisk, Margaret Cronin. "Billion-Dollar U.S. Verdicts Vanish After Appeals, New Rulings," Bloomberg News, January 8, 2009. Available online. URL: http://www.bloomberg.com/apps/news?pid=20601127&sid=a3pNSz7zXQ Tk&refer=law.

Glaberson, William. "A Study's Verdict: Jury Awards Are Not Out of Control," *New York Times*, August 6, 2001. Available online. URL: http://www. nytimes.com/2001/08/06/us/a-study-s-verdict-jury-awards-are-not-out-of-control.html.

Greenhouse, Linda. "For First Time, Justices Reject Punitive Award," *New York Times*, May 21, 1996. Available online. URL: http://www.nytimes. com/1996/05/21/US/for-first-time-justices-reject-punitive-award.html.

Greenhouse, Steven. "Searle Backs Medical Device," *New York Times*, October 9, 1985. Available online. URL: http://www.nytimes.com/1985/10/09/ business/searle-backs-medical-device.html.

Hamilton, Walton H. "The Ancient Maxim Caveat Emptor," 40 *Yale Law Journal*, 1931, pp. 1133–1187.

Harris, John F., and William Branigin. "Bush Signs Class-Action Changes Into Law," *Washington Post*, February 18, 2005. Available online. URL:

http://www.washingtonpost.com/wp-dyn/articles/A35084-2005Feb18.
html.

Holmes, Oliver Wendell, Jr. "The Path of the Law," 10 *Harvard Law Review*
457, 1897. Available online. URL: http://www.constitution.org/lrev/owh/
path_law.htm.

Langton, Lynn, and Thomas H. Cohen. "Civil Bench and Jury Trials in State
Courts, 2005." U.S. Department of Justice, Bureau of Justice Statistics,
2008. Available online. URL: http://www.ojp.usdoj.gov/bjs/pub/pdf/
cbjtsc05.pdf.

Manchisi, Francis P., and Lorraine E.J. Gallagher. "A Nationwide Survey
of Statutes of Repose," March 2006. Available online. URL: http://www.
wilsonelser.com/files/repository/NatlSurveyRepose_March2006.pdf.

Margolick, David. "G.M. Verdict Intensifies Debate on Jury Awards," *New
York Times*, February 6, 1993. Available online. URL: http://www.nytimes.
com/1993/02/06/us/gm-verdict-intensifies-debate-on-jury-awards.html.

McQuillan, Lawrence J., et. al. "Jackpot Justice: The True Cost of
America's Tort System," Pacific Research Institute, March 2007. Avail-
able online. URL: http://www.legalreforminthenews.com/2007PDFS/
PRI_2007JackpotJusticeFinal.pdf.

Mintz, Morton. "A Crime Against Women: A. H. Robins and the Dalkon
Shield," *The Multinational Review*, January 15, 1986. Available online.
URL: http://multinationalmonitor.org/hyper/issues/1986/0115/index.
html.

"National Rifle Association Ranked No. 1 on FORTUNE Power 25 List,"
Business Wire, May 14, 2001. Available online. URL: http://www.
allbusiness.com/government/elections-politics-politics-political-
parties/6122748-1.html.

Oregon Law Commission. "A Report to the Statute of Limitations Work
Group Regarding Statutory Time Limitations on Product Liability
Actions," July 2000. Available online. URL: http://www.willamette.edu/
wucl/pdf/olc/statutes_limitations_report.pdf.

Peck, Robert S. "A Time for Facts, Not Overblown Anecdotes," RAND
Review, Summer 2004. Available online. URL: http://www.rand.org/
publications/randreview/issues/summer2004/44.html.

———. "Defending the American System of Justice," *Trial* 18, April 2001.

Presser, Stephen B. "How Should the Law of Products Liability be Harmonized? What Americans Can Learn from Europeans," Manhattan Institute for Policy Research, Global Liability Issues, February 2002. Available online. URL: http://www.manhattan-institute.org/html/gli_2.htm.

Property Casualty Insurers of America. "*Tort Tax* Hurts Americans Even More Than Previously Thought," *PCI News*, March 27, 2007. Available online. URL: http://www.pciaa.net/publish/web/webpress.nsf/eaab008f9ddd474f862569df0065e618/86256bf40081c83b862572ab005435dc/$FILE/PCI%20TortTax-PRI%20Study.pdf.

RAND. "Punitive Damages in Financial Injury Verdicts." Available online. URL: http://www.rand.org/pubs/monograph_reports/MR889/MR889.text.html.

Rubin, Paul H. "Tort Reform Saves Lives," *Wall Street Journal*, October 8, 2005. Available online. URL: http://online.wsj.com/article/SB112873085838663424.html.

Rustad, Michael. "In Defense of Punitive Damages in Products Liability: Testing Tort Anecdotes with Empirical Data," 78 *Iowa Law Review* 1 (1992).

Schuler, Peter. "Inconsistencies Evident between the Monetary, Moral Judgments of Juries," *The University of Chicago Chronicle*, March 28, 2002. Available online. URL: http://chronicle.uchicago.edu/020328/sunstein.shtml.

Shanley, Michael G., and Mark A. Peterson. "Posttrial Adjustments to Jury Awards," RAND ICJ Report, 1987. Available online. URL: http://www.rand.org/pubs/reports/R3511/.

Springen, Karen, and Mary Hager. "Silicone: Juries Vs. Science," *Newsweek*, November 13, 1995. Available online. URL: http://www.newsweek.com/id/104075.

Umbright, Emily. "Report Finds Products Liability Cases on the Decline," *Daily Record* (St. Louis, Mo./St. Louis Countian), July 10, 2006.

U.S. Department of Justice, Bureau of Justice Statistics. "Tort Trials and Verdicts in Large Counties, 1996," August 2000. Available online. URL: http://www.ojp.usdoj.gov/bjs/abstract/ttvlc96.htm.

U.S. Department of Justice Report: Civil Justice Statistics for 1996. Available online. URL: http://www.ojp.usdoj.gov/bjs/civil.htm.

Viscusi, W. Kip. "Liability," *The Concise Encyclopedia of Economics.* Available online. URL: http://www.econlib.org/library/Enc1/Liability.html.

Walsh, David. "Tort Reform: Necessity or Myth?" *Wisconsin Business Alumni Update*, June 2005. Available online. URL: http://www.bus.wisc.edu/update/june05/tortreform.asp.

Web Sites

American Law Institute (ALI)
http://www.ali.org
> Organization founded in 1923 to provide clear and up-to-date information about American laws for lawyers, judges, and others. It provides periodic restatements on various areas of law, including torts, contracts, property, etc.

American Tort Reform Association (ATRA)
http://www.atra.org/
> This organization offers articles and reports in favor of reforming tort laws.

The American Trial Lawyers Association (ATLA)
http://www.theatla.com/
> This national group is made up of the top 100 lawyers from each state. Members must receive an invitation to join.

Cato Institute
http://www.cato.org/
> This non-profit think tank promotes libertarian principles of "limited government, free markets, individual liberty, and peace." The Web site includes numerous publications on product liability and other tort issues, among other topics.

Common Good
http://commongood.org
> This non-profit, non-partisan legal reform coalition conducts polls and hosts forums as it gathers information and viewpoints from experts on law, public policy, education, and other national concerns.

Heritage Foundation
http://www.heritage.org
> This conservative policy research organization's Web site contains articles on product liability in its Legal Issues section.

National Federation of Independent Business (NFIB)

http://www.nfib.com/

Located in Washington, D.C., this organization focuses on the interests of small businesses in the United States.

Public Citizen

http://www.citizen.org/

This non-profit consumer advocacy group's Web site includes news and publications relating to product liability.

RAND Institute for Civil Justice (ICJ)

http://www.rand.org/icj/

RAND's Web site contains research materials, reports, articles, and statistics relating to product liability as an area of civil law.

PICTURE CREDITS ⫸

144

A

accident rate trends, 65
Adams v. Bullock, 24
Agent Orange, 96
American Home Products Corp., Axen v., 93–94, 103
American Law Institute (ALI), 26, 29
American Tort Reform Association (ATRA), 28, 57
asbestos, 31, 95, 110
assumption of risk, 20
ATRA (American Tort Reform Association), 28, 57
attorneys
  criticism of, 118
  fees of, 110–111, 118
  sanction of, 119
automobile gas tanks, 35–36, 57
awards. *See* damage awards
Axen v. American Home Products Corp., 93–94, 103

B

Barnett v. la Societe Anonyme Turbomeca France, 96
Biomaterials Access Assurance Act, 28, 39, 47
Bloomfield Motors, Inc., Henningsen v., 26
BMW v. Gore, 80, 85, 87, 96, 103
Brandeis, Louis, 53–54
Brown v. Kendall, 21
Buick Motor Co., MacPherson v., 22–23
Bullock, Adams v., 24
Bush, George W., 108

businesses
  costs of product liability to, 36–37, 57–59, 73–75. *See also* liability insurance premiums; litigation costs
  federal bias toward, 50–51
  product liability in corporate decision making, 76
  strict liability as disincentive to expand and innovate, 60–62, 73–75
  uniform liability standards and, 42–43

C

Campbell, State Farm Mutual Auto Ins. Co. v., 47, 103
Cardozo, Benjamin, 22–24, 56
case law, 17
caveat emptor, 17–18
children's product safety, 66
civil law courts, 16
Class Action Fairness Act, 29, 43, 107–108
class-action lawsuits, 29, 32, 43, 106–108. *See also* mass torts
Clinton, Bill, 28, 34
Coca-Cola Bottling Co., Escola v., 25, 78
coffee burn lawsuits, 11–15, 16–17
collateral source issues, 117–118
Commerce Clause of U.S. Constitution, 40–42
common law, 17. *See also* English common law
compensatory damages, 16

Congress, and uniform liability standard development, 37–40
Consumer Product Safety Improvement Act, 66
consumer safety
  punitive damages and, 91–92
  uniform liability standards and, 40
consumers. *See also* plaintiffs
  liability litigation costs passed along to, 59
  negligence of, 56, 62–63. *See also* contributory negligence
contingent fees, 110–111, 118
contraceptive products, 61–62
contract law, 19
contributory negligence, 20, 31, 56, 62–63
corporate decisions, liability and, 76
cost-benefit analysis, 24
costs of product liability. *See also* damage awards
  liability insurance premiums, 27, 57–58, 75
  litigation costs, 36–37, 58–59, 73, 75
  overview, 16, 27
  strict liability and, 55, 57–59, 73–75
  in U.S. vs. other countries, 58
courts, consumer protection and, 52–54
Crier, Catherine, 62–63, 69, 110, 113

D

damage awards
  amounts of, 73

historic increases in, 57
limits on, 86–90
in marketplace
competitive balance,
77–78
damages, types of, 16
*Daubert v. Merrell Dow
Pharmaceuticals,
Inc.*, 21
deep pocket rule, 114
defect
court interpretation
of, 56
legal definition of, 30
defendant's rights, puni-
tive damages and,
82–84
defense arguments,
30–31
double compensation,
117–118
drug manufacturers,
61–62, 78–79
due care, 21
due process, 82, 83
duty to warn, 27, 30,
67–69

E

economic benefits of
uniform liability
standards, 40–43
economic effects. *See*
costs of product
liability
economic (monetary)
damages, 16
English common law,
18–19, 81
Escola, Gladys, 25
*Escola v. Coca-Cola Bot-
tling Co.*, 25, 78

F

Fairness in Product
Liability Act, 28
federal agencies, and uniform liability stan-
dard development,
37–40
federal bias toward busi-
ness and manufac-
turers, 50–51
federal liability laws. *See*
uniform liability
standards
federal preemption
defense, 31, 50–51
federal standards adher-
ence, and punitive
damages, 98–99
Feinstein, Dianne, 107
Fen-Phen lawsuit,
105–106
Ford, Gerald, 51
*Ford Motor Company,
Grimshaw v.*, 97
foreseeable risk, 21–22,
30
forum shopping, 43–44
fraud, 18, 19, 24
French Commercial
Code (1807), 18
functional products
liability analysis, 29

G

GDP. *See* gross domestic
product
General Aviation Revital-
ization Act, 39, 47, 61
*General Electric Co. v.
Joiner*, 116
global competition
safety of U.S. products
and, 76–77
strict liability costs and,
58, 59
uniform liability
standards and, 42–43
Gore, BMW v., 80, 85, 87,
96, 103
*Greenman v. Yuba Power
Products, Inc.*, 26, 79
*Grimshaw v. Ford Motor
Company*, 97

gross domestic product
(GDP), tort costs as
percentage of, 58

H

Hamilton, Walton H.,
18
*Haring v. New York and
Erie Railroad Co.*, 21
*Haslip, Pacific Mutual
Life Insurance Co. v.*,
82, 103
Heflin, Howell, 49
*Henningsen v. Bloomfield
Motors, Inc.*, 26
Hilliard, Francis, 19
history of product liabil-
ity, 17–27
Holmes, Oliver Wendell
Jr., 33

I

Industrial Revolution,
19–20
inequity of treatment,
35, 37
injury and death rate
trends, 64
innovation, potential
liability as inhibitor
of, 60–62, 75
insurance. *See* liability
insurance
international competi-
tion. *See* global com-
petition

J

*Joiner, General Electric
Co. v.*, 116
joint and several liability,
114
judge-made law, 17
judges, in punitive dam-
ages assessment, 91,
100–101
jurisdiction, forum shop-
ping and, 43

K

Kendall, Brown v., 21

L

la Societe Anonyme Turbomeca France, Barnett v., 96
labeling. See warning labels
law of product liability. See product liability law
The Law of Torts, or Private Wrongs (Hilliard), 19
Levine, Weyth v., 78–79
liability insurance premiums, 27, 57–58, 75
liability insurance, uniform liability standards and, 37
liability lawsuits, trends in numbers of, 72–73
Liebeck, Stella, 11–12, 16–17
litigation costs
  misleading figures on, 73
  as percentage of GDP, 58–59
  strict liability and, 75
  unpredictability and, 36–37
litigation tax, 59
Lopez, United States v., 46

M

MacPherson v. Buick Motor Co., 22–23
marketplace competitive balance, liability compensation and, 77–78
mass torts, 43, 108–113
McCain, John, 34
McDonald's coffee burn lawsuit, 11–14, 16–17

McDonald's obesity lawsuit, 111–112
McMahon coffee burn lawsuit, 14–15
Medical Device Amendment, 39, 51
Medtronic, Inc., Riegel v., 39
Merrell Dow Pharmaceuticals, Inc., Daubert v., 115
Model Uniform Product Liability Act (MUPLA), 27–28, 34
monetary awards, limits on, 86–90. See also punitive damages
monetary damages, 16
Multiparty, Multiforum Trial Jurisdiction Act, 39, 47
MUPLA (Model Uniform Product Liability Act), 27–28, 34

N

Nader, Ralph, 76
National Childhood Vaccine Injury Act, 47
negligence
  as basis for compensation, 20
  contributory, 20, 31, 56, 62–63
  not required under strict liability, 25, 29
negligence standards, and court administrative costs, 75
New York and Erie Railroad Co., Haring v., 21
noneconomic damages, 16, 81

O

ordinary care standard, 21

P

Pacific Mutual Life Insurance Co. v. Haslip, 82, 103
Personal Responsibility in Food Consumption Act, 112
pharmaceutical industry, 61–62, 78–79
Philip Morris v. Williams, 83
Pinto lawsuits, 96, 97
plaintiff arguments, 29–30
plaintiffs
  negligence of. See consumers, negligence of; contributory negligence
  strict liability ensures fairness toward, 77–79
  unfair advantage of, under strict liability, 56–57
Priest, George L., 87
private aircraft industry, 39, 60–61
product costs, liability litigation costs and, 59
product liability law
  history of, 17–27
  overview, 15–17, 32
  reform of, 27–29
Product Liability Reform Act, 63, 85–86, 89
product lifespan, 63
product safety
  and global competition, 76–77
  punitive damages and, 96–99
  strict liability and, 64–67, 75–77
Protection of Lawful Commerce in Arms Act, 39, 47

punitive damages
  argument against,
    summary, 80–82, 92
  argument for,
    summary, 93–94, 104
  constitutionality of,
    101–103
  and consumer safety,
    91–92
  and defendant's rights,
    82–84
  as deterrent, 96–99
  exaggerated reports of,
    94–96
  frequency of awarding
    of, 95–96
  goals of, 16, 82
  judges in assessment of,
    91, 100–101
  juries in assessment of,
    32, 90–91, 99–101
  limits for, 86–90
  reduction of, 96
  standard of proof for,
    85–86

R
reform of class-action
    litigation, 106–108
reform of product liabil-
    ity laws, 27–29
remittitur, 91
res ipsa loguitur, 25, 29
Restatement (Second) of
    Torts (1965), 26
Restatement (Third) of
    Torts (1997), 29
Riegel v. Medtronic, Inc.,
    39
Roman law, 18

S
safety. See consumer
    safety; product safety
safety improvement
    trends, 64
scientific testimony,
    114–116

silicone breast implants,
    115
State Farm Mutual Auto
    Ins. Co. v. Campbell,
    47, 103
states
  consumer protection
    and, 52–54
  uniform liability
    standards and, 38
states' rights, 45–49, 52
statutes of limitation,
    36, 116–117
statutes of repose, 36,
    116–117
Stevens, John Paul, 80
strict liability standards
  argument against,
    summary, 55–60, 70
  argument for,
    summary, 71–72, 79
  consumer benefits of,
    77–79
  consumer negligence
    and, 56, 62–63
  and duty to warn,
    67–69
  economic effects of, 55,
    57–59, 73–75
  exaggeration of
    problems with,
    72–75
  innovation and
    business expansion
    impacts, 60–62,
    73–75
  and product safety,
    64–67
  and promotion of
    public safety, 75–77
  and unfair plaintiff
    advantage, 56–57
strict product liability
  as legal argument, 29
  theory of, 26–27
successor liability,
    113–114

T
tobacco lawsuits, 108–
    109, 111
tort, defined, 16
tort law, 19–20
tort reform, 50
tort tax, 59
Traynor, Roger J., 25,
    78, 79

U
unavoidable harm, 20
Uniform Commercial
    Code (UCC), 17
uniform liability stan-
    dards
  argument against,
    summary, 45, 54
  argument for,
    summary, 34, 44
  case law tradition and,
    49–50
  Congress and
    federal agency in
    development of,
    37–40
  court and state
    legislature in
    consumer protection,
    52–54
  economic benefits of,
    40–43
  in elimination
    inefficiency and
    unpredictability,
    34–37
  federal bias toward
    business and
    manufacturers, 50–51
  forum shopping and,
    43–44
  reform efforts and,
    27–29
  states' rights and, 45–49
United States v. Lopez, 46
unpredictability, deter-
    rent effect of, 76

U.S. Constitution, Commerce Clause, 40–42
U.S. Supreme Court
  on constitutionality of punitive damages, 102, 103
  on states' rights in citizen protection, 52
  on states' rights in interstate commerce, 46

V
vaccines, 38–39

W
Walsh, David, 48
warning labels, 27, 30, 40, 67–69, 78–79
warranty of quality, 18
Wyeth v. Levine, 78–79
Williams, Philip Morris v., 83

Winterbottom v. Wright, 19
Wright, Winterbottom v., 19

Y
Yuba Power Products, Inc., Greenman v., 26, 79

VICTORIA SHERROW is a freelance writer and a member of the Society of Children's Book Writers. She is the author of many books for middle and high school readers, including several titles in the POINT/COUNTERPOINT series.

ALAN MARZILLI, M.A., J.D., lives in Birmingham, Ala., and is a program associate with Advocates for Human Potential, Inc., a research and consulting firm based in Sudbury, Mass., and Albany, N.Y. He primarily works on developing training and educational materials for agencies of the federal government on topics such as housing, mental health policy, employment, and transportation. He has spoken on mental health issues in 30 states, the District of Columbia, and Puerto Rico; his work has included training mental health administrators, nonprofit management and staff, and people with mental illnesses and their families on a wide variety of topics, including effective advocacy, community-based mental health services, and housing. He has written several handbooks and training curricula that are used nationally—as far away as the territory of Guam. He managed statewide and national mental health advocacy programs and worked for several public interest lobbying organizations while studying law at Georgetown University. He has written more than a dozen books, including numerous titles in the POINT/COUNTERPOINT series.